The Gift of Tears

Keith Nano

The Gift of Tears

A Terrifying Illness
A Miraculous Healing
An Extraordinary Journey

Keith Nano

Evergreen
PRESS

Mobile, Alabama

ISBN 978-1-58169-696-7
For Worldwide Distribution
Printed in the U.S.A.
Evergreen Press
P.O. Box 191540 • Mobile, AL 36619
800-367-8203

Contents

Acknowledgments

This book is dedicated to all the souls who marched in Jacob's Army. You blessed us in ways that cannot be measured, can never be sufficiently thanked, and can never be repaid.

It is dedicated to the men and women of UMass Memorial Hospital in Worcester, Massachusetts, and of Boston Children's Hospital, and to doctors and nurses everywhere who are the hands and feet of Jesus, and the vessels for miracles.

It is especially dedicated to my bride, Alethea, who is easily the most wonderful woman on the planet.

And it is dedicated to Jacob. Go see what the Lord has planned for you, son.

Introduction

I know no secrets. I hold no authority. I stake no claim to any measure of scholarly or spiritual wisdom. I'm an ordinary man. There are many more things in this life which I cannot explain than those which I can. My story and my convictions are no one else's, nor do I expect them to be. I deny no man the right to believe whatever he chooses or the right to walk in whatever direction his heart leads him. I don't presume my opinions or beliefs have any more importance than anyone else's. I respect the individual, personal discoveries and conclusions about life and faith formed by other people, based upon their own experiences.

Each man's life is a uniquely private and individual journey of discovery. What one uncovers and experiences during that journey, how they interpret it, and what it reveals to them, ultimately carves their character, shapes their worldview, and molds their heart. Each man's reality is his own. One man's luck is another man's fate. One man's wish is another man's prayer. One man's coincidence is another man's miracle.

This book chronicles a physical and spiritual trial faced by a family in Massachusetts, a family different from, but as universally the same, as any other. It's the story of a sick boy named Jacob and his incredible healing. It's the story of a miracle. It's also the story of the heartening enlightenment of a father and an entirely different kind of healing. It's a story of brotherhood and community. It's a story of darkness, light, and hope. It's a story of the impact of charity, kindness, and love during times which so frequently seem to be governed by selfishness, violence, and hate.

As is always the case, readers will come to their own conclusions based upon what has been etched in their hearts. For me, the pages that follow present a shining accounting of the goodness in the human heart, the power of prayer, the wonder of miracles, and the mystery of faith.

By His wounds, we are healed.
Isaiah 53:5

PROLOGUE

IT ALL MATTERS

I was a quirky and cerebral lad when I was a boy. From a very young age, I was astonished by nature and science. I was a lover of the outdoors and spent quite a bit of time outside, exploring my own little corner of the world. This place happened to be a blue collar, middle-class neighborhood on the shores of Whalom Lake in Lunenburg, Massachusetts.

Growing up on a lake presented innumerable quests for an inquisitive and adventurous young mind. I spent nearly as much time in the water as I spent out of it. There was an antiquated amusement park on the lake. Every five minutes for the first half of my life, I heard the creaky chain of the rickety wooden roller coaster hoisting its passengers up to the top, followed by the shrieks and screams of its passengers as they plummeted down the first drop. The park has long since vanished, but the echoes remain. It was a terrific kid's neighborhood.

I wasn't a loner by any stretch of the imagination, yet I was just as content to be by myself in the woods or on the pond as I was hanging around Whalom Park, riding bikes, playing sports, or finding mischief with other neighborhood kids.

I was fascinated with dinosaurs. After dinner, when the table was cleared, my Dad and I would often draw panoramic scenes of volcanic landscapes containing as many types of dinosaurs as we could fit onto a poster board. No detail was spared. When my little mind drifted, I often pondered a world without people running around in it and imagined being the only human in a prehistoric land. I was equally captivated by snakes. Much to the dismay of my mother, who more than once was caught off guard by a shadowy and slithering motion in the house. I caught them, played with them, and made them my pets.

I was a dreamer, and as a youngster, I was determined to follow my fascination with dinosaurs and snakes. A budding scientist, I read every book that I could get my hands on. I decided I would grow up to become either a paleontologist or a herpetologist at an age when I'm confident I probably shouldn't have been able to properly pronounce those words. In fact, around the time I was seven years old, I wrote a letter to the author of my favorite snake book to ask him what I needed to do to become a herpetologist. I was serious. I could identify every snake on every page in the book, and for the most part, I had their Latin names committed to memory as well.

I painstakingly wrote the letter in my best printing on crisp, green, double-lined paper, which I heisted from school in my Speed Racer lunch box. I made every letter the perfect width and height. I used a ruler to cross the "t's". I wanted to appear mature and to demonstrate how serious and grown up I was, oblivious to the fact that a correspondence from an adult would be typed, or at least written in cursive, and that it wouldn't be written on green paper with gigantic dashed lines. A thoughtful response from the recipient of the letter informed me that the author had passed away. I was discouraged, but I wouldn't be derailed. There were discoveries yet to be made.

After dinosaurs and snakes, my entomology phase came along. No insect, arachnid, or other creepy-crawly was safe. Many met their untimely demise in my freezer where I'd place them in Dixie cups, so I could later carefully study them, compare them to the photos in my books, identify them, and wonder in amazement at their tiny and masterful complexities. My wonderful mother was less than pleased from time to time at her unexpected frozen discoveries. My next-door neighbor, Miss Becky, a kind and benevolent soul who seemed to me to be a hundred years old, often let me wear one of her gardening coats. It was white and hung well past my knees. Much to my thrill, she afforded me unrestricted access to her garden to hunt whatever I could find. She called me her little professor.

Perhaps my constantly wondering mind was to blame for the insomnia I suffered as a child, and which still plagues me today. Falling asleep was always a chore and often impossible. My best sleep typically came in my school classes after lunch, where I would generally pass out daily. Insomnia and an analytical and inquisitive young mind proved to be a challenging mix.

In my continual study and observation of nature, and with an insatiable appetite for the wonders of the natural and scientific worlds, I gobbled up every wildlife television show and every science and nature documentary and book that I could. I was determined to be a natural scientist. I traveled to every corner of the world through the pages of my books. At night, I imagined. The discoveries would be endless.

I wasn't raised in a house of faith or religion, and I knew little of those realms. What I did know, and what I learned from a very young age, was that one could either be a person of faith, or they could be a lover of science. Everything I learned had taught me that faith was unreasonable, not based on fact or reality, and it contradicted science and reason. I learned from my surroundings, my teachers, my books, and my documentaries that to be intelligent was to eschew faith. I learned that to embrace a secular belief system was the hallmark of reason and intellect. To do otherwise was to be less than intelligent. Indeed, it was to be scoffed at and even ridiculed. Although I was by default a Naturalist and an Evolutionist, this presented a significant issue for me.

The notion that being a lover of science precluded me from embracing faith didn't sit well with me, although I wasn't at all sure why. I always felt as if something was missing, as if there was some unfinished equation I needed to solve. I didn't know at the time exactly what was troubling me, but later in life I'd realize precisely what it was.

Something tugged at me night after night in the moonlight of my boyhood bedroom as I lay awake, tracing shapes on the wall with my fingers and contemplating the cosmic questions in my young mind. I vividly recall sitting up straight in my bed one night as I suddenly realized that nothing in the entire world mattered.

I realized that I believed, or at least I acted as if I believed, that there was nothing special about being a human being. According to the books I read, I was nothing more than a pile of carbon. I came to the sobering conclusion that, since that was the case, in the grand scheme of things, it really didn't matter what I did, what I believed, whom I would love, whom I would hurt, what I would become, where I would go, or what I would do. None of it mattered. I concluded that I was no different than a lion, or a snake, or a daisy. I would live, and I would die. There was ultimately no meaning to any of it. For reasons far beyond my ability to grasp at the time, it made me profoundly sad. I'd reached my unhappy conclusion based upon what the secular world had ingrained in me. I had a very limited understanding of God and faith, but I was aware that there existed a perspective and a worldview which differed from the only one I'd ever really been exposed to.

In my studies of prehistoric eras and unimaginable spans of geological time, I soaked in every word that told me the earth and the universe had been around for billions of years. I accepted that people were inconsequential, insignificant, and accidental blips on the chart of history. From my books I had learned that the universe appeared, developed, and flourished for reasons unknown and unexplained, and all the unfathomably intricate fine-tuning necessary for us to exist happened simply due to chance.

Despite all the magnificence I studied in nature, and despite the awe-inspiring design, detail, and beauty that I discovered, I absorbed every jot and tittle that proclaimed it was all without design and, therefore, without purpose. Those were the facts as taught to me. But something just didn't seem right.

I came to the stark realization that if what I thought I believed were true, and if I and everyone I knew and loved were really nothing more than accidental assortments of coincidental atoms, and that if there were no such thing as a soul, or a Creator, or a heaven, then nothing really mattered at all. I reasoned that if there is nothing when I die, then there was really nothing to begin with. I tried to imagine nothingness. I couldn't do it. I could think. I could dream. I could ponder. I could plan. I could communicate. I could wonder. I could understand. I could see and hear and feel and taste and smell.

Yet when it came time to die, according to conventional wisdom, all that would instantly change, and there would simply be nothingness. I would cease to exist, and I concluded that nothing about me when I'd been alive would ultimately ever have truly mattered at all. My existence, when all was said and done, would've been no different had I been a weed that emerged from a crack in a sidewalk, which was plucked and discarded. I couldn't wrap my mind around that idea.

As I grew older, I was fully in tune to the idea that evolution was a scientific fact and that there was no God and no need for Him. I adopted the worldly approach that faith in a Creator was less than sensible. Still, something consistently didn't make sense to me, and I remained unable to sort it out in my mind.

Throughout the years, my life's path would expose me to some of the darkness in the hearts of men. Over time, the idea that nothing mattered would be reinforced time and again by such things that can harden a man and cloak love, kindness, and peace behind a sullen cloud. During those years, however, what perplexed me as a youngster, leaving me with a gnawing feeling of incompleteness, would eventually come into clearer view.

As I broadened the array of the books I read, I would eventually learn about the faith-based concept of every person having a "God-shaped hole" in their heart. I was exposed to the notion that we each have an emptiness inside, which can only be filled and satisfied by God, whether we realize it or not.

Throughout my life, I'd tried to fill the hole with many other things, but nothing fit, and nothing filled it. At times I felt shackled, jaded by the prevalent awfulness of a broken world and what appeared to be an inherent absence of goodness in people. I questioned humanity. I questioned purpose.

Despite the absence of faith in my life, I was magnetically drawn to the concept of who Jesus Christ was. I'd heard friends talk about Him and I'd been to church a handful of times. Something in me wanted to know Him and to understand more, but I didn't want to be unreasonable or unintelligent. I would struggle throughout my late childhood and into adulthood mired in this quandary.

All my life I thought along the lines of what had always been instilled in me. I wondered how anyone could believe in something they couldn't see or touch, something for which there existed no evidence. I scoffed at the idea that someone could believe in something that hadn't been witnessed. After all, creation couldn't be proven, and it couldn't be replicated. It couldn't be scientifically tested. No one had ever seen it. There was no empirical evidence. It was entirely a matter of dependence upon faith. And faith was silly. In my self-righteous simplification of the matter, I derisively dismissed the Creationist as being someone who foolishly believed a

wild story they'd read in a book. My personal sense of reason, however, wouldn't allow me to escape the incredible irony.

When my mind was sharp enough to further dissect what had
been pulling at me for years, I realized that I was fully embracing
evolution, the cornerstone upon which the entire foundation of
Naturalism is built, the linchpin which hinges together an entire
worldview, and without which it all falls apart. Yet, I developed an
uncomfortable awareness that, despite the very things for which I
criticized the Creationist, neither could evolution be seen or
touched. It had also never been witnessed. It could also not be
proven, replicated, or scientifically tested. For every alleged proof,
there was an equally compelling rebuttal if one sought to find it.
There was no real empirical evidence. Yet, exactly as the
Creationist did, I believed what I believed because I read it in a
book. This profound irony stoked fires within me.

I finally began, at least in my own mind, to solve the self-imposed riddle that plagued me for years. I concluded that
Naturalism, no different than the belief in special Creation, was
entirely dependent upon faith. One could either have faith that
everything came from nothing and for no reason, completely by
chance, or they could have faith that they were specially created
with purpose. Either way, each position required a giant leap of
faith. This forced me to evaluate things using an entirely different
calculus. Armed at last with the intellectual dexterity to at least
begin to more thoughtfully navigate this lifelong quagmire, my
heart found new direction.

The more I learned about life, nature, and science, and about
the world and the universe in which we live, the closer I drew to
God. I began to attend worship services in the military and became
friends with Christians who spoke to me about their faith. My
Christian education came largely in the form of a cowboy named
Don from Brownsville, Texas. We were stationed together in the
Philippines, and when we weren't being crazy, young airmen in the

United States Air Force, Don was telling me about Jesus Christ. He carried a Bible everywhere, and I asked him constant questions, tagging along with him like I was a ten-year-old with his high school brother.

As I look back, it seems that the Lord was revealing Himself to me one little piece at a time. Over the course of many years and through many experiences, a foundation of faith was being laid, whether I recognized it or not. In 1991, not long after I returned from the war in the Persian Gulf, deeply convicted, I finally gave up anything left in me that held Jesus at arm's length. Everything welled up inside of me, and I was stopped in my tracks. There in the dusty laundry room of a tired military barracks, with my heart and mind at peace, I prayed a prayer of salvation and surrendered my heart to Jesus. My spiritual journey, which had unknowingly begun when I was a very young boy, could now move forward.

Years of inner turmoil would boil down to one thing for me—either we as human beings were created, or we weren't. It seemed there existed no other reasonable alternative. If we weren't created, if we just happened, then I figured nothing mattered, never did, and never would. If, however, we were in fact specially created, then logic demanded that there was a Creator and, therefore, a purpose. In that case, I figured that everything mattered more than I could possibly fathom.

What I discovered throughout my life revealed to me that despite everything I'd learned to the contrary, science and faith were not mutually exclusive as is so often presented. I found more and more that, in my opinion, science unequivocally supported the notion of special creation, intricate design, and purpose. The science was sound. The facts were stubborn. The varying dynamic, I decided, wasn't the evidence. Evidence doesn't vary. What varied was the interpretation of the evidence.

I finally concluded that faith wasn't, in fact, rebuked by science, but rather it was rebuked by the hearts of men. I would come to fully accept that I was wrong when I concluded that nothing mattered. I began to wholeheartedly believe that everything matters.

It all matters.

ONE

A MAN IS RESCUED

I met my wife in a bar in August 1997. It wasn't glamorous. I was a young man of twenty-seven years who played third base for a local, rag-tag softball team in Leominster, Massachusetts. After our games, most of the team would usually head from the ball field to a local sports bar called Legends to shoot pool, drink pitchers of beer, regale one another with our own versions of the game we'd just played, and make excuses as to why we were relegated to knee-brace softball instead of playing for the Boston Red Sox. On a hot summer evening after a game, one of my softball chums introduced me to a female friend, whom I found to be very attractive. She invited me to meet her the next evening. I thought it was a date, but I was evidently mistaken.

Not long after I arrived, it became clear that the girl I went to meet was far more interested in another guy. I wasn't going to stick around for that, so I sauntered into an adjacent room where I found two beautiful ladies throwing darts. Carefree and a little cocky, and since I was clearly now free for the evening, I insinuated myself into their dart game.

I was especially drawn to one of them. She was gorgeous with smiling eyes and an infectious laugh. I was immediately taken by her. After opening flirtations, requisite superficial conversation, and a few dumb one-liners, I asked her name. She told me her name was Alethea. I'd never even heard the name before. I had to have her repeat it and I sounded it out. Ah-LEE-thee-ah. She told me it was a Greek name, meaning truth. The beauty of her name fit the woman who was smiling at me. On the outside I kept my cool. On the inside I was saying, "Wow!"

We played darts all night. We talked. We drank beer. We laughed. We had a great time. It was one of those nights a young man hopes never ends. On my way home, all that night, and the following day, I kept thinking, *Wow! She's awesome.* Two days later, after thinking about Alethea from the minute I'd left her, I decided I needed to see her again. Few forces are as strong as that which drives a guy to want to know if a girl he's interested in reciprocates his sentiment. I wasn't feeling patient, and there was no way I was just going to wait to bump into her again by chance.

I had to wait at least one day, though, because unwritten man code dictated that contacting her right away would constitute some form of desperation. So, I impatiently waited one very long day. Then I took the risk that a guy always has to take, sooner or later, when he's pursuing a woman—that of being perceived as being either very sweet or a little creepy.

Without really thinking it through and driven by the desire to see her again, I went to Alethea's workplace unannounced. During our conversation the night we met, I'd learned that she was the manager of a children's clothing store in a nearby mall about half an hour away. So I drove there, somewhat questioning what the heck I was doing.

I confidently strolled into her store with a purpose. I walked right up to her and asked her out while she was hanging clothes on a rack, right in the middle of the store. Asking a girl out is no different for a guy when he's twenty-seven than it was when he was twelve. It's like trying to balance yourself as you walk across a creek on a fallen log. It's really not complicated at all, but there's so much room for error.

I could tell she was a bit shocked that I was there. I wasn't at all sure whether it was good shock or bad shock since all we really knew was each other's name, and any chemistry I thought I might have detected could well have been the result of alcohol-induced delusion. Initially I was convinced that I'd made a huge mistake.

She didn't say a lot. She kept shuffling hangers and turned to a couple of her co-workers with an indecipherable smile as if she were silently asking them what to do. They giggled and then pretended they were busy and not listening. Much to my relief, though, she lifted her eyes, smiled at me, and said yes. I'd made it across the log! It's entirely likely that I skipped out of that mall like I'd just won the lottery.

On our first date, I took Alethea to dinner at a local pub called Slattery's in the neighboring city of Fitchburg. We talked, and we seemed to connect from our very first words. There was no awkwardness. I took a big risk right out of the gate. Not long into our dinner, while we were minding our manners, measuring our words, and beginning to peel away the outermost layers of our masks as we felt each other out, I asked Alethea how she felt about children. She lit up and told me she loved children. She told me she couldn't wait to have children of her own and that she'd always dreamed of being a mom and having a family.

"I adore kids!" she said.

"Good. Because I have one," I replied.

I guess I wanted to get it all right out there, rather than to build something up that was doomed to fail. I recognized that it can be a deal breaker in the dating world when you already have a child. I pulled out a photograph of my four-year-old son, Dominic, and handed it to her. I was paying close attention to her reaction. She didn't ask for the check. She didn't stealthily put her sweater on, move toward the edge of her chair, or eye the closest exit. And she didn't say that she just remembered she had to call her aunt about something.

She was genuinely engaged in the subject. She told me she wanted to be married to the right man and have lots of kids. My friends would later joke that most guys would've run away screaming if a girl said something like that on a first date. I wasn't going anywhere, though. We hit it off fabulously for the rest of the evening. By the end of our first date, there was no doubt we'd be spending more time together.

After that night, we spent every minute together we could. On our second date, we went out to dinner and when I walked her to my car and opened the door for her, we shared our first real kiss. After that, we pretty much never stopped kissing. It was surreal how we seemed to know we were meant for each other, and we both had a sort of "Where have you been all my life?" attitude. It was something special. When we were at our respective jobs, we couldn't wait to see each other at the end of the day; and when we did, we ran to each other like we were in a Humphrey Bogart movie. A deep connection existed between us. I fell head over heels for her. It was the romance of my life.

We were a strange, but perfect, match. I was loud; she was quiet. I was outgoing; she was shy. I was adventurous; she was careful. We weren't even each other's physical type. I'd always been particularly attracted to shorter brunettes, yet Alethea was tall and blondish. She preferred a tall, athletically slender type, and a city guy. I was a short, thick, blue-collar dude who only went to Boston if I was going to Fenway Park or Logan Airport. I felt far more comfortable in blue jeans and a ball cap than I ever was in a shirt and tie.

Despite Alethea being young, beautiful, successful, and smart, and despite the fact that she could have arguably had any man she wanted, she chose me. There are times these days when she's less than pleased with me for one reason or another, and I like to remind her of that.

After a short period of time, Alethea met my folks at a gathering of friends and family. I introduced her to my dad, and they sat down at a picnic table to chat. I was hoping my father wasn't being too goofy, something he had a penchant for. They talked for what seemed like an hour. When they were done, I walked over to my dad, who inexplicably called me Butch from the time I was five. After having only just met her, he looked at me quite seriously and said, "You'll be marrying that one, Butch."

Her folks also accepted me. Her mom referred to me as the "keeper," evidently indicating it was alright if I stuck around awhile. I loved Alethea's family from the outset, and their Christian values played no small role in getting me back on track after I'd been spiritually wandering for some time. Alethea's mom, Lisa, would become like my second mother, and I love her dearly.

I'd had a terrible time with my divorce from Dominic's mother. I had met her while I was in the military. We dated, and she got pregnant. When it came time for me to either leave the Air Force or to re-enlist, I decided that if I was going to have a family, I wasn't going to do the military thing and move from place to place. I'd lived in the same house on the same street in the same town all my life. I was someone who valued roots. A transient family life didn't appeal to me. So I took my pregnant girlfriend home, found a cheap apartment, landed a job, and we later got married unceremoniously in a downtown office.

Dominic was born when I was just twenty-two. His mom was even younger. We were only kids ourselves. Still, I was a young man of vision. I had a house built in rural Hubbardston, Massachusetts, and away we went. I had it all planned out. I had a good job, a new home, and a new family.

It all came crashing down, though, in only a few short months. It was no one's fault. It just was what it was. We were so young. We split up, and I ended up living out of a suitcase on my best friend's couch. John, a friend that I considered my brother and the guy who'd been my closest buddy and partner in crime since the seventh grade, took me in and helped me through what was, to that point, the most difficult time of my life.

I never thought divorce would happen to me. I was a good guy. I wasn't perfect, but I was a hard worker and an honorable man. I was crushed, I was mad, and I was confused. I responded with reckless abandon. I cursed God. I didn't understand. I wasn't ever much of a drinker, yet I began hitting the bars frequently, partly just to have something to do other than to wallow in my misery, partly hoping to find another woman to be with, partly to escape what was occurring, and partly to be around my pals who might help keep me grounded and prevent me from doing stupid things. It wasn't just on the weekends. I was closing bars on Monday and Tuesday nights. It was a recipe for disaster. I was showing up at work in the mornings in rough shape. I'd lost focus. I'd lost faith. I was a mess. I wasn't headed in a good direction.

I dated some, but it was like learning to breathe again when Alethea came into my life. It seemed to be mutually understood that we'd spend the rest of our lives together. Alethea rescued me. She helped save my life in many ways. I often thought to myself that it was no coincidence our paths had crossed. I'd strayed far from my true character and from what I knew was right. She helped bring me back. I felt as if God sent her to me. I had new purpose and a new heart for the Lord.

I saved up enough money to rent my own place, and I relieved John of his best-friend duties of harboring a fugitive. I rented a small apartment just big enough for me and Dominic, who stayed with me on an irregular basis. Alethea had an apartment across town. One night, long before we ever officially discussed marriage, I was picking her up at her place. She was still showering and getting ready for wherever it was we were headed. I was sitting in her kitchen and saw a stack of assorted papers, bills, and a notebook in the middle of the table. In true snoop fashion, I did what any guy would do and flipped open the notebook and leafed through the pages.

In her handwriting I saw that she'd been writing Alethea Nano, which was odd since her name was Dudley. It was written five or six times. She'd been practicing writing what would be her married name. On another page were the names of several people I didn't know, yet they also had my last name. It turned out they were the names she was choosing for the children we'd have.

In a moment of serendipity, the telephone rang. I glanced down the hall, and Alethea was clearly still occupied in the bathroom, so I answered it. It was her previous boyfriend. I could tell by the extended pause that he was caught off guard by the fact that a man had answered her telephone, and understandably so. I told him she was busy. He asked if I'd tell her that he'd called and if I would tell her to call him back when she wasn't busy. Holding the list of our future children's names in my hand, and perhaps motivated by a bit of testosterone-driven bravado, I said, "I'm pretty sure she'll be busy for a while."

In less than a year, Alethea and I joined forces, rented a condominium in Leominster, and began our life together. I proposed to her under the fireworks at Coolidge Park in Fitchburg on July 4, 1998, not quite a year after we first met. I'd had the ring for some time. I didn't want her to find it, and I'd learned that she was as snoopy as I was when it came to things like that. So, I put it in the only place I figured she'd never look—the trunk of her car. One look at the state of her car and anyone would understand why I wasn't worried about her finding it. She smacked me when she realized she'd unknowingly been driving around for weeks with her diamond only a few feet away from her.

Each day we learned a little more about each other's personal story and where we were with respect to our individual spiritual journeys. We were both Christians, and we talked about our faith. We attended worship services together in a very small church in

Leominster. It wasn't even really a church. Services were held in the basement of a Boy Scout building.

We grew together in love and in Christ. We were married by our pastor in Clinton, Massachusetts, on May 2, 1999, on as beautiful a spring day as anyone could imagine. It was a joyful and special day complete with a nervous groom and a painfully stunning bride. After honeymooning in Costa Rica, we embarked on the routine of life as a young, married, blue-collar couple.

The joy of our wedding day was surpassed only by the day when Alethea announced she was pregnant. She was married, and now her family was about to begin. She was happy. We gave my parents a gift bag on Christmas day 1999. They were sitting on the couch in the family room when they opened it to find a pair of baby booties, one blue and one pink. I was able to snap a photograph a few seconds later at the precise moment when their faces lit up as they digested the meaning of the gift. It's one of my favorite pictures.

Jacob arrived eight months later, on August 16, 2000. He wasn't originally going to be named Jacob. Some weeks earlier we'd decided on the name Owen. Everyone knew we were having a baby and the name was going to be Owen if it was a boy. Except that when Owen was born, and when we looked at him for the first time, we both agreed that he wasn't Owen. He was Jacob. It was as simple as that. So, there was our son, Jacob Erik Nano.

Alethea had a younger brother named Erik. I learned during our courtship that he'd been tragically killed a few years before we met. They lived adjacent to an Army base in Lancaster, Massachusetts. Naturally, being an intrepid young boy, Erik ventured (as any boy would) onto the base to explore. One day he found some unexploded mortar shells and placed them in his backpack. One of them detonated. He was sixteen years old. Alethea made sure that her brother lived on in her son's name.

Alethea was never as happy as she was when she was holding

her baby. As clichéd as it may sound, she was made to be a mom. She is singularly the most selfless and benevolent person I've ever known. She adored Jacob. He was a beautiful and healthy baby. Everything was perfect. Less than a year and a half later, Nicholas arrived. The next year, after looking at what seemed to be every single house in Worcester County, we found a nice little one in Gardner, Massachusetts, in a family-friendly neighborhood. It was 2003 during the housing market spike, and we paid ridiculously too much for the modest little house. It was immediately a struggle just to pay the mortgage, but we had our home. Five months later, Isabella arrived. Two years after that, little Samuel completed our family. By 2005 we had four children who were five years old and under along with Dominic, who was now a teenager. Life was busy.

I'd served as a cop when I was in the Air Force. More specifically, I was a Military Working Dog Handler. I had initially aspired to translate those skills and experience to the Massachusetts State Troopers when I eventually left military service, but after I separated from active duty, with a baby on the way, I couldn't wait. I needed to take the first opportunity I found.

The Department of Correction soon offered me a job as a corrections officer. No one grows up saying they want to work in a prison, but you take what you can get when you need to pay the bills and raise a family. I took a temporary job with the Massachusetts D.O.C. with the intention of using it as a stepping stone on my path to the Troopers. But by the time Samuel was born, time had passed by and I'd been with the Department for thirteen years. So much for it being a temporary job. It was now my career.

With a crazy job and a crazy home life, it was sometimes difficult to keep up. I often quipped that I found it was easier to deal with murderers, gang-bangers, and riots at the prison than it was to manage four toddlers. Handling all the kids and managing the home came far more naturally to Alethea than it ever did for me.

After nearly twenty years of serving my country and the Commonwealth of Massachusetts—all of them working in emergency professions—there was little that could really rattle me. Between my time in the Air Force and the Department of Corrections, I'd served at various times as a cop, a K9 handler, an EMT, a member of special response, search and rescue, and tactical teams, a corrections officer, and an investigator, and I'd been to war.

Even though I was young, I was reasonably sure that I'd seen it all. It's now my opinion that no one has seen it all until they've had four kids who are five years old and under. That could rattle even the heartiest soul.

Still, Alethea was the type who could be nursing one baby and holding another and see a newborn on television and say, "Oh…I want another one." Quite to the contrary, when she asked if I wanted to have more kids (and she did), I told her, with only a mild amount of sarcasm, that I'd rather be back in a foxhole in the desert. I'm decidedly more surprised that I survived those toddler years than anything else in my life.

We had no more children.

Two

COACH DAD

Jake was a great baby and toddler. He was happy and healthy in every way. He was the epitome of a bouncing baby boy. It was clear from an early age that he'd be an athlete. As soon as he could walk, it seemed, he began to run around the house full speed repeatedly declaring, "I'm a fast runner!" He never stopped. I accommodated and encouraged him. He was my buddy. If I had to guess, he was probably about three years old when I taught him how to swing a bat for the first time and began tossing him Wiffle balls.

When I came home from work, he'd be waiting on the front steps with bat and ball in hand, perpetually sporting a Boston Red Sox hat or jersey, or both. When we broke for dinner, I could rest assured that when I was done eating, he'd already be waiting to head back outside. We played ball every day. It was our ritual. I'd often throw him pitches until it was dark. We used flat stones from the flower bed as bases, and the lawn had permanent base paths where no grass would grow. If I had a nickel for every pitch I threw to Jake, I'd be a wealthy man.

Sometime when he was around four years old, I bought him his first baseball glove, and that was all she wrote, as the saying goes. Jake was a baseball guy. He was a natural. Fatherly pride aside, he had uncanny skills for a young boy. We soon graduated from Wiffle balls to baseballs. I taught him to field grounders properly, how to get under fly balls, how to use his body and his legs to swing the bat. It gave me great joy to teach him the game I loved.

When tee-ball started, it was the first time many of the other kids had ever even picked up a baseball. Jake, comparatively speaking, was rather seasoned at that point. There were many occasions when he smashed another kid in the head with the baseball because he expected them to be able to catch it like I did when he threw it to me. I had to tell him he needed to toss the ball more softly than he did when he and I were playing. When it came to hitting, while the newcomers struggled to simply make contact with the baseball sitting atop the tee, Jake was slamming it in such a manner that I had to back the other kids up. It was almost as if he were saying, "Let's be done with this small time tee-ball stuff already and play some real baseball!"

I coached Jacob (and Nicholas) throughout Little League. It was one of the greatest pleasures of my life and something I truly miss. It was a privilege I cherished, and one that I took very seriously. Sometimes I probably took it too seriously—not in the sense that I was one of those dads who coached as if their nine-year-old boys were vying for the American League pennant, but in the sense that I really wanted to be a good coach.

I often asked my wife if I was being a good coach, for fear of failing to live up to the role. I'd had both great coaches and poor coaches at different times during my life, and I wanted to be the antithesis of every lousy coach I'd ever had. I remembered my good coaches, and decades later, I still recall specific things they did or said. I wanted to be a good enough coach that my kids would remember the things I taught them.

During my coaching years, I'd routinely drive home from work through traffic on Route 2 westbound, all the while drawing up a batting line-up and figuring out my pitching rotation for the game. Coaching wasn't always easy, but it was always interesting. Invariably, during my game planning, I'd receive the call from the mom whose kid suddenly needed a ride that night, or from the dad who would ruin my finely tuned line-up by telling me his son couldn't play because he had a tooth pulled that day or for some other reason.

There was always a fly in the ointment, just to make it interesting. I'd frequently have to shoot home or call my wife for whatever it was I'd forgotten that was crucial to the game. It was always something—the bat bag, my sunglasses, a pencil, my hat, my pitch counter, or sunflower seeds. Like clockwork, at least one kid would usually forget his hat or glove. There were many times I had to dispatch my wife to drive across town to save the day in whatever manner was necessary in time for the game's first pitch.

Coaching was always hectic, and I always seemed to be in a rush. Sometimes I'd show up and find no umpire. Then I'd have to begin the bevy of phone calls necessary to find one. Once or twice I went to the wrong field in my haste. I even had the wrong day a time or two and realized it only after I'd dropped my chalk lines and raked the infield and noticed it was awfully quiet and no one else had shown up yet, including my own kids. I'd call Alethea and ask her what day it was, and she'd laugh at me. It was a lot to do, but I loved every minute of it. For all the times I cursed it, I miss it tremendously.

I was involved with Little League baseball in spring and early summer, and then for a couple seasons I coached a Jimmy Fund team for the second half of the summer. We played Fall Ball into the autumn if there were enough kids to field a team left over from the ones who turned to football that time of year. We were a baseball family. Jake always had a baseball in his hand. When I flip through family photos, it's difficult to find a picture of him without a baseball, a bat, or a glove.

My neighbor and close chum, Tim, was a baseball guy too. He'd join us and toss the ball, throw pitches, or hit grounders and fly balls. We lived side by side. His yard was bigger than ours, so we were usually over there. By the time Jake was eight or nine years old, he mastered the art of tracking a fly ball. Tim and I would hit or throw high pop flies to him, and we'd do it at such an angle that Jake would have to track it and dive to catch it. It was recreation for us to watch him lay out flat. He dove with a child's abandon that was just plain fun to watch.

We'd try to get the fly balls as far away from him as we could, yet close enough so he could just barely get there in time with a dive. Tim and I would hoot and holler each time, and we'd let out a "Whoa!" for every terrific diving catch. We were disappointed if we missed the mark and hit the ball so that Jake could catch it on the run without having to dive. He had the ability to track a fly ball well beyond his age.

Our wives, who were best friends, would sometimes go out for a while and leave us to watch all the kids, seven in total. They'd all run back and forth through our houses and the yards. I think we didn't do the best job of looking after everyone all the time. There were several times, after we'd hit or thrown what seemed to be our hundredth ball to Jake, one of us would suddenly realize we'd lost track of time and had no idea where the others were. We'd quickly find them, of course, and then laugh and start to play ball again. Alethea and Michele, upon returning home, would ask how the kids had been for us. "No worries. It was a piece of cake," we'd say.

Jacob grew into a fine baseball player. He lived and breathed baseball. When we got home from practice or a game and pulled into the driveway, Jake would hop out of the car, but he wouldn't go inside. He might have just returned from practicing or playing baseball for two or three hours or more, yet instead of heading inside to eat or rest, he'd run right into the yard and start tossing the ball off his pitch-back net.

He'd throw himself dozens of grounders and pop-ups. He had the knack of hitting the angles where the ball would come back at him so that he'd have to dive. We'd have to bark at him to come inside before he beaned himself in the face because it was getting too dark to see. I like to think he got it from me, but his mother was athletic too, so I'll have to share the credit. Sports were always going on in our home. It was predominantly baseball, but we also played football frequently, and during the winter it was pond hockey season.

We took great pains to keep a nice hockey rink throughout the winter on Whalom Lake. I'd been skating on Whalom since I was five or six years old. My lifelong friend, Randy, still lived there, along with several of my other childhood friends and my older brother, Eric, who still lived in the house where we grew up. Once the ice froze for the year, Randy and I and a few other hearty souls would be out there, in all conditions, clearing the snow, flooding and freezing the rink, and skimming the ice. We even had jerseys made for the WPHL—the Whalom Pond Hockey League. As forty-somethings, it was a joy for us to have our kids doing the same things we did ourselves from the time we were just lads. We'd put up lights and play until the last person had to go home, or until we were frozen solid, utterly exhausted, or both.

I started to teach Jake and Nick to skate probably around the time they were nine or ten years old or so, and they picked it up in no time. Our skating seasons were relatively short, dependent upon the weather, from the time the lake froze through mid-to-late February. Once the freeze took hold, we skated every chance we could.

There were many days I came home after a long day at work and was in no mood to head out into the cold and skate. But there were my boys when I walked in the door, dressed for hockey, skates in hand. Randy would announce on Facebook if the ice conditions were good for the night. Sometimes there was only a handful of us. Sometimes there were a dozen or more.

Jake had a Carolina Hurricanes hockey sweater that he loved (despite being a die-hard Boston Bruins fan). He was quickly dubbed "the Hurricane" by Randy and the other boys at the pond. Most everyone had a nickname. Mine was "Triple P", which stood for Pistol Packin' Pastor. It was my buddies' humorous way of referring to me as a faithful guy with a penchant for carrying a sidearm. The back of my WPHL jersey read "PPP" in lieu of my name.

One year we had an idea that began an annual tradition. After playing nearly every night for weeks, we'd have a tournament in February. Dozens of skaters would come, and we'd draw names for teams out of a hat. It was the highlight of the year for us. Another one of my lifelong friends, Sean, owned a nearby restaurant. For the annual tournament, Sean sent his staff down to the lake in one of his catering trucks, and they'd set up steam tables, grills, and kettles on the ice next to our rink. It was great fun. We'd skate and eat all day, no matter the weather. The winner of the double-elimination tournament earned a trophy, a hat, or a sweatshirt. More importantly, they won a year of bragging rights.

Jake pined for the time when he'd be old enough and big enough to play in the "big boy" tournament. We didn't play full contact, but neither did we play no contact, and there were certainly bodies flying, along with a bit of testosterone, so the young ones were typically spectators on that day. For the kids who weren't skilled enough to play in the tournament yet, we stopped half way through the day to  give ourselves a break and to let them play a game against each other. The kids' game was always one of the highlights of the day. In 2014 Jake would finally have the skills to play with the big boys in the WPHL Invitational, as Randy dubbed it. He couldn't wait for the pond to freeze. By Thanksgiving he gave me his prediction as to when the ice would be good. "We'll be on the ice by Christmas," he prognosticated.

Sports reigned supreme. Jake tried his hand at soccer. He was a standout and an exceptional goalie for the one season he played, but soccer didn't appeal to him, and he moved on. He tried cross-country and, again he shined, but that was too boring for him. At age thirteen he wanted to try football. He tried out and, to my surprise, made the cut for the local Pop Warner club called the North County Panthers. They were a powerhouse and perennial contenders. I didn't hold out much hope for him to be successful, as most of those kids had been playing organized football together since they were very young, and Jacob had never played. His only football experience was limited to running fly patterns on the street while Dad showed off his arm with a Nerf football.

Again, though, he was a natural. His aggressive personality was suited to football. Coaches felt he would serve well as a linebacker, and they were right. At first, he was only on the field for a few snaps each game as he learned the rules, the language, and the flow of the game, but he quickly earned his way to more playing time.

Although I loved the game and the thrill I got from watching him compete, I wasn't a big fan of my boy playing football. A friend of mine was paralyzed in a football game when I was in high school. The impact of experiencing that had never left me. So, although a huge football fan, I left it for others to play, and I didn't particularly want my boys to go in that direction for fear of a catastrophic injury. I was never one to hold them back from something they wanted to do, but I admittedly discouraged them from playing football.

Despite my initial reluctance and trepidation, Jacob flourished. He relished every opportunity to deliver a hard hit. One of the coaches pulled me aside one day and told me, "Your boy's got a ways to go, but he's got something you just can't teach." The Panthers marched through that season, defeating their opponents decisively and winning the state championship. Mom and I made it to nearly every game. They were within one game of heading to Florida for the big, televised national Pop Warner Championships when they were finally defeated in the Regionals.

Jake attended Overlook Middle School in the town of Ashburnham. We lived in the city of Gardner, but we sent him to the Ashburnham and Westminster School District under the school choice program. As an eighth grader, he was called up with a few of his classmates to the high school level to play on the freshman squad for the Oakmont Spartans, who were evidently short on players. He didn't see much playing time at all as a middle schooler on a high school team, but I think it was a good learning experience for him. I thought it would be healthy for his character to be one of the least skilled players on a team. I'd gone to great lengths to teach my boys humility. There were times I felt I'd been successful; but other times, not so much. Jake needed to work on being humble.

Our family life was demonstrably centered on athletics. It was baseball, football, hockey, basketball, soccer, cross country, and basketball for Jacob and Nicholas, gymnastics for Isabella, and soccer for Sam. We were busy. Our routine took us from one game to another, one field to another, and one town to another. My wife and I, like all sports parents, were largely relegated to playing the role of a taxi service. We were on the move seven days a week.

Sunday morning, though, was for church, a time during which I tried, oftentimes unsuccessfully, to slow things down and focus.

Coach Dad

THREE

FAMILY FOUNDATIONS

When we moved into our home in Gardner in 2003, I wanted
to check out local churches. Bethany Baptist Church was right
down the street from our new home. I began and ended my search
there. For a few Sundays, I attended worship services by myself before I decided to bring my family. I was conducting reconnaissance.
I wanted to know if there were any funny business going on there.
There wasn't.

I felt at home at Bethany. It was a small church with a largely
older membership of kind and welcoming people, and I found the
pastor to be compelling. Pastor Dan, a man who would become my
friend, mentor, and confidante, preached from the Bible. If it were
not in the Bible, it wasn't preached. I liked that. Dan was as passionate about the grace and love and mercy of the Lord as he was
humble in his own human fallibility. He was a selfless servant and a
strong, effective, and gifted spiritual leader. He earned my respect
over the ensuing years as I grew to know and love him. He would
be someone who would impact my life.

After my brief spy mission to the church, I brought my family,
and we were soon taken in as members. We now had our church
family, and we loved them. I served as a volunteer leader in the

kids' club, which was called All Stars for Jesus, and all our kids attended it. Alethea volunteered for various things as well, and for a time she coordinated the weekly Hot Meals program. As we grew in faith together as a family, I felt confident that the bricks of my children's foundations were being solidly laid.

Although my own family rarely attended church when I was a child, my mother had been raised Catholic, so I was baptized as a baby in a Catholic church in accordance with ritual and received my First Communion. But I had never been baptized into new life and been born again. Alethea and I were baptized together at Bethany, a solemn and reverent experience and a wonderful gift for a husband and wife to share.

A few years down the road, my friend and brother in Christ, Tom, approached me about serving as a deacon. I still considered myself a young Christian and felt woefully ill-equipped to serve as a spiritual leader for other people. I quite honestly found it challenging enough simply trying to lead my own family. I balked at the proposition, believing (and rightfully so) that I wasn't nearly qualified. But Pastor Dan astutely advised me that the Lord doesn't call the qualified. Rather, He qualifies the called.

I prayed about it. I felt the tug and the call, and I accepted the nomination and was elected to the position. I now sat on the Bethany Deacon Board with a group of fine and honorable men, each of whom I called my friend and brother. It was a responsibility I took very seriously, and as unworthy as I felt I was for such an honor, there I was. I had no question about my faith, but I had much to learn and far to grow.

During the following years, I'd often look out over the congregation when I was speaking or praying from the pulpit, and I'd wonder how on earth I ever got there. On one occasion I was leading Sunday worship service, and in the middle of speaking, I was stopped cold as I contemplated the fact that I was entrusted with bringing the Lord's word to people. There was a pregnant pause in my speaking, which was unusual for me as I'm an adept public speaker, typically very comfortable in front of people. I looked around at all the faces. At a loss for words, I remained caught in one of those awkward moments of searching for something to say when my mind had irretrievably wandered. I made eye contact with one of my fellow deacons seated in a pew in front of me. He returned a look as if to ask if everything was alright. I smiled and said, "I'm just amazed. If God can use me for this, He really can use anyone." There were some chuckles and a few amens. I still wonder how or why the Lord ever chose me, of all people, to help bring His word to other people.

It was important to me for my children to have a Christian foundation. Like any parent, I feared the perils they would face in the world. My own life experiences compelled me to teach them what I saw as truth. However, my children, in general, didn't devour the Word as I hoped they would over the years.

Of all my kids, Jacob seemed to have the biggest heart for Jesus, at least outwardly. He often asked me questions about faith, God, Jesus, and the Bible. He became a fan of the contemporary Christian music I listened to. We'd listen to our playlists every time we were in the car. Our favorite band was Casting Crowns. We knew every word to every song, and we sang our hearts out.

In the "little memories" category of life, one of my most cherished is the memory of driving around town with Jake while singing songs together. Once my wife bought us tickets to see the Crowns at the Lowell Auditorium. She and I took Jake and one of his friends from church. It was a tremendously powerful and moving worship experience, not to mention a stellar musical performance. I can remember looking at my son singing at the top of his lungs during the concert and thanking God for giving him a prayerful heart.

Our favorite movie was *Facing the Giants*. It's a powerful story of faith and resilience in the face of seemingly insurmountable obstacles and steep odds, juxtaposed with a sports theme. It's a compelling and particularly moving film and, in my opinion, one of the best sports movies ever made. We watched it together many times. Faith and sports were two areas where Jake and I always found our common ground.

Jacob also shared my love of writing. Like me, he was always writing songs and poems. There were notebooks in every corner of our house and in both bathrooms with his writing in them. It elicited a warm feeling in my heart when I'd pick up a random notebook or a piece of paper and find a song of praise and worship written by my young son.

My hope was that my children would walk through life guided by Christian values and principles, not only for the obvious eternal reasons but also in the hope that they would avoid the paths which I knew, all too well, frequently scarred and destroyed lives. I often saw my own sons in the faces of the young men with broken lives that I saw every day in prison. When awful things happened in the prison, I often thought to myself, *That's someone's son.* I tried to imagine what it's like as a parent to have a son in prison.

I felt a deep personal conviction that Christian values would provide my children the safest path, and I hoped in my heart that they would each grow to love the Lord and to be born anew with Jesus Christ. So it was a comforting joy for me every time I heard Jacob singing in the shower about Jesus, instead of singing the latest song about drugs, booze, guns, or money.

I tried to get my boys to various places where they could flourish outside of, and in addition to, the constant sports which dominated their days and their seasons. Most of those opportunities would prove to be cost prohibitive for us, as we were never in the best financial shape. At various times, though, Dominic, Jake, Nick, and I managed to get away. Dominic and I once attended a spectacular father/son adventure camp in the Rocky Mountains of Colorado. Nick, Jake, and I went to a great father/son getaway at

Monadnock Bible Camp in New Hampshire, and they attended some seasonal camps at Berea Christian Camp, also in New Hampshire. They were all rewarding experiences. It was harder to tell, though, with the others than it was with Jake. Nicholas, for example, was our quiet one. He talked about as much as a potato.

That wasn't the case with Jake—he never stopped talking. He was outspoken, opinionated, and strong-willed. He always had something to say. He always thought he was right, and he always wanted to be in charge. As much as he aggravated me on a regular basis with his immature application of those traits, coupled with the resolute stubbornness that his mom so graciously handed down to him, I recognized that one day they would serve him well when he matured and learned to harness and regulate them. From an early age, Jacob seemed destined to be a leader of men.

It was also important for me to help my children develop servants' hearts. As often as I could, I would try to demonstrate to them the principles of loving thy neighbor. I'd have them assist with setting up and serving holiday meals at the church for the less fortunate in our community. I would deliberately let them see me clear the snow off the driveways of neighbors who weren't home during a storm or help someone with their groceries. I encouraged them to befriend kids in school who might be loners. I often left them in the morning, telling them to find some way to be a blessing to someone that day, or I would challenge them to be kind to someone for no particular reason. I wanted my children to be givers in this world and not takers.

Hurricane Sandy barreled up the east coast from the Caribbean in late October 2012. It left a devastating swath of destruction in its wake after it smashed into New Jersey and New York. Those areas had only just rebuilt after Hurricane Irene. The damage was enormous, and dozens lost their lives across eight states. After seeing the widespread destruction on the news, I consulted the Deacon Board and we decided to call some churches in the affected areas and see if they needed help. The very first call I made connected me with the pastor at First Baptist Church in Freeport, New York, who was coordinating relief efforts. Freeport had been hit with a nine-foot storm surge, and the destruction was extensive. The pastor responded to our offer of help with a resounding yes!

When I asked what we should do and what we should bring, he told me to bring as many men and tools as I could find, and he asked how soon we could get there. I called my boss and asked for a week of vacation. Over the course of the next several days, some of the other deacons and I gathered a group of men and figured out some logistics. Jacob and I, along with eight other men, piled into a few cars with enough clothes to last several days and as many tools as we could carry and headed out to Long Island.

It was a fantastic trip full of prayer, good will, fellowship, male bonding, father/son time, and people helping people. The church was a hub of activity, and we arranged ourselves in cots as temporary squatters. The pastor coordinated with people and agencies in the community to address various needs. Our team ended up being tasked with demolition. We proceeded to tear down multiple homes, right down to the studs, so the owners could rebuild. The flood damage was immense. The floodwater lines in some of the houses were well over six feet high. Everything was lost. So many people's homes were laid waste and were now filling with mold and other assorted nastiness. All their worldly possessions were heaped on the curbs, lining every street and corner.

I'd witnessed destruction and loss before, but for Jake, it was an awakening. It was a tremendous opportunity for him to experience the feeling, the privilege, and the obligation of serving and helping his fellow man. Other than the inevitable fallout of walking around in New York for several days dressed in Red Sox gear, which was basically all Jacob wore, it was a very rewarding experience and a precious time for me with my son, for which I was very thankful.

I desperately wanted to teach Jake (as with all my children) to be a giving, honorable, kind-hearted, and noble person. One of my greatest personal fears had always been failing as a father by not effectively teaching my kids to be all those things. I always strove to teach them love, manners, dignity, fair play, patience, turning away wrath, charity, helping others, being the difference, standing up for what's right even if it's unpopular, and standing up for anyone, whoever they may be, who couldn't necessarily stand up for themselves. I wanted my sons to grow to be good men.

There may have been times I preached too much. Rolling eyes have often revealed to me that I can be painfully redundant in my lesson teaching with my children, and I know there were many times when I was teaching or lecturing them that they just wanted me to shut up. Even when I coached baseball, I didn't just coach baseball, I tried to coach life as well, not only with my own boys but also with my other players. I always drew parallels between baseball and life.

Baseball is a terrific metaphor for life. It was just as important to me that I was teaching young minds about how to deal with life as it was that I was teaching them how to lay down a drag bunt. My sons would complain that they had to hear the same things both at home and on the ball field.

I loved all my baseball kids, and I found coaching Little League to be of great personal reward. Many of the Little League boys, including my son Nick, were moving onward and upward after our 2013 season. As it would turn out, my last game as a baseball coach with the Gardner Phillies would be a tough loss during the playoffs, ending our final championship run. Although I tried not to let on to anyone, I was very sad that it appeared my coaching days were numbered.

The boys who would remain in Little League knew my time was done because Jake already moved up to the Babe Ruth level the year before, and now Nick would be moving on. After that game, one of my players who I was particularly fond of, came up to me while I was loading the team gear into my trunk after my final post-game speech and after we'd already said our goodbyes. He was crying.

Ever the coach, I put my hand on his head and told the young lad to toughen up and keep his chin up. I told him that a loss is a loss and that they played their hearts out. I told him that I was very proud of him and that there's no crying in baseball. He stopped me dead by saying, "I'm not crying 'cause we lost, Coach. I'm crying 'cause I can't play for you anymore."

To this day, that was one of the best things anyone has ever said to me. Sometimes, when we think no one's paying attention, they really are. It meant a lot to me. I guess I was a half-way decent coach after all. When it came to my own kids, however, I often felt that I fell short.

The love I felt for my children was reflected in poems I'd written over the years. I enjoyed writing poetry from a very young age. I found an ability to express myself through words, and some of the most joyous (as well as some of the darkest) experiences of my life jumped from my heart and onto the paper over the years. I'd written special poems for each of my children. I wrote Jacob's poem shortly after he was born when he was still an infant. He was our first child, and the sense of joy and responsibility Alethea and I shared ran deep.

Cradle

(A Prayer for Jacob)

The Lord gave us a gift in you
Beyond what we understand
Perfectly formed in the love of the womb
Sculpted by His own hand

As from seed to stalk you ripen
You will be our garden to tend
And by light or by shadow of darkness
Our fortress to defend

You will drink from the well of our faith
A solemn challenge of our being
And be fed at the breast of the Word
That it may raise you into seeing

In acceptance of this precious charge
We will cradle you in prayer
That the One who conceived you in miracle
Would guide you as His heir

That within His robe you be gently swaddled
To be counted among His flock
That you may grow to be His likeness
And He to be your rock

The sweetness of your arrival
Could be surpassed by one joy alone
If He who delivered you would bless us
By keeping you as His own

When I read the words today, it seems almost as if I knew when I wrote them that there would come a time Jacob would need to be cradled by the Lord. The notion that he would need to be held and defended through times of darkness, indeed, would prove to be prophetic.

Jacob had a heart for the Lord, and I coached and fathered him to the best of my limited ability, but he also had some demons to fight. Of all my children, Jacob and I seemed to be the most connected in faith, despite our many battles. In addition to being my most faithful child, though, he was also my most challenging in a number of different ways. As often as I wanted to strangle him when he pushed my limits, we always had baseball and faith to bring us back together. The pre-teen and early teen years were not easy years for Jake or for our family. Our faith and resilience were tested often and sharply. The obstacles and trials were many. It became more important than ever for me to keep my children, and Jacob in particular, rooted in faith.

Sports, school functions, family functions, kids' club, friends, birthdays, sleepovers, deacons' meetings, prayer meetings, volunteering, along with my more-than-full-time job, kept me going at a dizzying pace. I can't imagine how it all worked. There weren't enough hours in a day.

There were times I felt as if I were spread so thin that I didn't know if I was coming or going. I would frequently joke with my wife that I could be Tom Hanks' character in the movie *Castaway* and not complain about it one bit. But for every time I'd wished I could somehow be stranded alone on a deserted island for a while, I counted my blessings. I loved my wife, my kids, my job, my ball players, my family, my friends, and my church. But just as surely as I loved it all, I would often ask God to slow me down somehow.

He did.

Four

Dominoes Falling

In recounting my life's experiences, I always look for the way the Lord may have moved in them. Series of events have often seemed to me like lines of dominoes falling. Sometimes they fell straight and true, but other times they branched off in many directions. When unlikely occurrences in my past seemed to connect themselves in meaningful ways, I often drew a parallel to the methodical cause and effect of a falling trail of dominoes. Something rather unremarkable usually served as the impetus or the first domino; yet as unexceptional as it may have been unto itself, it often ultimately had the power to set in motion a chain of events that gained ever-increasing momentum and frequently had far-reaching effects.

For every major life event I examined, one after the other, more dominoes cascaded through a twisting, turning, circuitous route in my mind. They'd either have fallen exactly the way I expected they would, or they took me in entirely unexpected directions. Sometimes, one domino would be out of line ever so slightly, causing a complete halt and a need to re-set.

I've often marveled at significant events in my life and traced them back to what I felt were rather insignificant beginnings. In what would eventually prove to be the most profound series of events in my entire life, the first domino to set many others in motion would be, of all things, a tick.

On an early December morning while I was getting ready for work, I was in the shower and felt something on the side of my thigh. Lo and behold, there was a tick attached to my leg. This wasn't entirely unusual for me. Between my regular fishing excursions (which typically included long walks through the woods) and cutting trees for firewood, I was certainly no stranger to ticks. I found ticks crawling on me or my clothing fairly frequently. It was rare, though, that I'd had one become attached and embedded so that it needed to be pulled out. It was also at least a little unusual, I thought, to have picked up a tick in December in Massachusetts. It must have hitched a ride while I was in the woods doing my lumberjack duties.

Each year I cut down trees in the woods on the property belonging to my buddy, Tom. I used a wood stove to heat my home, and Tom had innumerable trees he wanted removed, so it was a mutually beneficial arrangement. I'd been knocking down trees and cutting them up for firewood in the woods surrounding Tom's property for several years. In the fall and early winter, I would typically spend many days cutting the trees down, then chunking, splitting, hauling, and stacking the wood before the snow got too deep and the temperatures too low. It was always hard work, but it was also a welcome and necessary alone time for me. I would spend hours there, sometimes all day.

I found a certain solace when I was lost in the hum of my chainsaw or the back-and-forth of my wood splitter. I'd spend much of the time thinking, meditating, or singing my favorite songs. I thought about life, love, and family. I thought about work, debt, and death. Sometimes I worked out problems. Sometimes I prayed. Other times, it seemed, not a single organized thought passed through my mind.

From the time I was a child, I'd always found comfort in the woods. When my chainsaw or splitter would run out of gas, I'd usually find a stump, take a break, sit for a while, and take a few moments to soak in the beauty I always discover in nature. To me, nothing is quite as peaceful as a late autumn breeze creating a symphony of a million instruments in the trees. Sometimes I'm silent; sometimes I'm not. I'm sure Tom's lovely wife, and my dear friend, Joanie caught me belting out some of my favorite tunes on more than one occasion while she was tending to her garden.

My wife never quite understood my need for solitude. She marches to the beat of a different drum. Perhaps our differences are part of the glue that always holds us together. Where I seek solitude, she seeks company. She turns on all the lights in the house while I follow her around and turn them off. When she heads to the city, I find a forest trail. She never does anything for no reason and rarely by herself; I perpetually search for things to do alone, away from crowds, and often for no specific reason at all.

I like to nap; she doesn't. She's a planner, while I'm anything but. She's one of those people who inexplicably think that countertops are places to actually put things, whereas I spend all day clearing them off. She always wanted to go to Disney. To me, the idea of going to a ridiculously expensive and crowded place in hundred-degree heat with screaming children, only to wait in long lines to get on a ride designed to make me vomit, represented the seventh level of hell. Our differences are many.

I drive places without necessarily having a destination. I tend to go out with no specific plan in my mind with the understanding that I'll figure out where I'm going when I get there. Sometimes I just need to think. Sometimes I need quiet. Sometimes I need to listen to a particular song. Oftentimes, much to her aggravation, I purposely escape to my car when she runs upstairs for something, so I can avoid her asking me where I'm going and the subsequent look I get when I tell her that I have no idea.

She can't grasp the notion of getting into the car and taking off with no specific destination. One of the most frequent text messages she sends to me is, "Where did you go now?" Sometimes I do it intentionally just to get a rise out of her. I smile when I eventually receive her text message, which I always know is coming.

When I discovered the tick on my leg, I realized it'd been there a while. It dawned on me that for the previous couple of nights after I'd gone to bed, I'd been fiddling with it prior to going to sleep, thinking it was a pesky skin tag or something. Ticks don't typically bother me, although in this case, I was a bit concerned. Other than being ugly and gross, they weren't much of a problem unless they were attached for an extended period, in which case a person is more susceptible to contracting Lyme disease. When I realized it was a tick I'd been picking at, I knew it had been there at least two days, so I was concerned about Lyme. At any rate, I had Alethea remove the tick, and I got ready for work.

———⊰◆⊱———

At that time in late 2014, heading to work meant I was heading for the Massachusetts Correctional Institution at Concord, known as MCI Concord, in Concord, Massachusetts. After twenty years of working my way up through the uniformed ranks of the agency, I'd taken a stab at an opportunity to move to the management team. Following an interview process, I was selected and promoted to the position of Director of Security at MCI Concord, and I transferred there in the summer of 2012. So, I'd been at MCI Concord for a little more than two years at the time.

It was a good job, and I worked with many fine people. In retrospect, it was a much-needed change for me that, for a number of reasons, came at the right time in my life and my career. When I was selected, I had mixed emotions. I was less than enthused about my new commute, which was twice the distance I'd traveled for my first twenty years. I wanted to do something different but was also a bit nervous about going to a new facility as one of the bosses where I wouldn't know most of the people. I always welcomed a challenge, though. It turned out to be a blessing in many ways.

As the Director of Security, more than two hundred staff members reported to me, including officers, sergeants, lieutenants, and captains. As with most of my endeavors, I took the responsibility of my position seriously. I strove to be a positive and effective leader, though I'm sure there were times I failed. I'd had some bosses in the past who were somewhat disengaged. So, I strove to know who my staff members were as people and not just as employees. I took a personal interest in their lives.

Consequently, I spent a lot of time talking with my staff. I knew some of them already, as I'd worked with them at different times in other facilities over the years, but I also made new acquaintances and ultimately formed many new and lasting relationships. Of them, none was more notable than my relationship with a fella by the name of Steve. He was bold, opinionated, and animated. He had a booming baritone voice that resonated throughout whatever room he was in. If Steve was in the room, you knew it.

When you first show up at a prison as a new administrator, you have hundreds of sets of eyes on you, watching your every move and sizing you up every minute of the day. I had hundreds of staff members and about a thousand inmates. That's a lot of eyes. Like everyone else, Steve sized me up awhile to see what I was all about.

I spoke with him daily, not only to get to know him as one of my key staff members but also so he could help me to learn the nuances of the operations of the facility for which I was now responsible. As we became more familiar, we loosened up a bit and became more informal with one another, as is usually the case. I always enjoyed my conversations with Steve.

During our daily discussions and interactions, I must have

made periodic references to church. Or perhaps I'd made comments about God or spirituality. One day, Steve and I were having a routine conversation when he abruptly interrupted and declared, "I gotcha, Boss! You're a believer! Aren't you?"

I wasn't sure exactly what I'd said to elicit such a response, but I replied, "Well, yeah. Why?"

Steve let out a laugh like he was the guest of honor at a surprise party and hollered, "I knew it! I've been waiting for you!"

I wouldn't know what he meant by that statement for some time to come. In any event, there was this big, burly guy that I'd only known for a few weeks, giving me a hug. I would later learn that Steve served as a pastor at a large church in Fitchburg. I thought it was at least a little unusual that a full-time corrections officer was also a pastor. Being brothers in Christ gave us a common bond that would serve as the cornerstone of the friendship we would develop.

Naturally we did our jobs, but when time permitted, we engaged in passing conversations about life, love, faith, family, and prayer. We were boss and employee, but we also became friends. Any given conversation with Steve could turn on a dime from a prison incident, to the weather, to the New England Patriots, to a Bible study. It wasn't uncommon at all for us to politely discuss, or to heartily debate, our individual interpretations of a Bible passage, of human behavior, politics, good, evil, or anything else for that matter. We had very busy jobs and much work to do, but we could usually pack a heck of a conversation into a few minutes' time. I looked forward to going to work each day at Concord, and Steve was one of the reasons why.

It wasn't unusual for Steve to come barreling into my office with a head of steam and with two or three other people to say, "Check this out, Boss...." After which he would apprise me of the subject of discussion they'd been debating or dissecting. Sometimes it was just about the newest offensive lineman on the New

England Patriots. Sometimes it was a bit deeper than that. Sometimes I had input and cheerfully offered my two cents before telling them to get back to work. Other times I'd say, "Well, you're the pastor, Steve, you tell me!"

There was a group of Christians who worked at the prison, and we frequently talked when time and circumstances would allow. To me, it felt like positive energy in an inherently negative environment.

At the end of nearly every conversation, Steve would smile and say, "You're awesome!" It was his trademark comment. It wasn't that he thought that I was particularly awesome. Steve thought everyone was awesome, and he liked to tell them that. No matter who you were, he thought there was something about you that was awesome. Steve was a bright soul. He loved his fellow man in a Christ-like fashion.

I would eventually come to see Steve as one of the most prayerful and faithful people I'd ever known. He had an unabashed love for the Lord, and he praised Him loudly and openly. He witnessed the Gospel with a passion. He traveled to the other side of the globe on mission trips to bring Christ's message to all corners. He welcomed debate and skepticism. He was a transparent, kind, and thoughtful person. At work I was his boss, but spiritually, I was undeniably his subordinate. His cryptic comment of having been waiting for me would find its way to the back of my mind. In due time, however, it would re-emerge in a most powerful way.

After Alethea removed the tick from my leg, I went to work like I did on any other day. By the end of the day, though, I had enough of a limp that people at the prison were asking me what was wrong. I'd always been one of those people who stayed at work far too long when something was wrong, or if I was sick. I usually had to be told to go home. It's a work ethic thing I pride myself on, and I've often told my coworkers and colleagues that unless I'm bleeding from my neck, in the hospital, or dead, they can expect me to be at work.

One of my captains, John, gave me a hard time as my limp grew worse. John and I were friends, and we'd come up through the ranks together. Professionally he was my right-hand man at the prison as the Shift Commander of the day shift. I could count on John more than any other person. We'd served as prison block officers together when we were youngsters in the agency. We'd often reminisce about our youthful antics and indiscretions and marvel at the fact that we were now command staff members charged with the operation of a major secure facility. He was a salty veteran, a tremendous leader, and a firm, fair, and good man. Although he reported to me in the chain of command, he was more a friend than he ever was a subordinate.

John saw that my leg was hurting and pulled me over. He said, "Look, sometimes it's time to just go home. Get the hell out of here. Go see your doctor."

I was in a bit of pain and agreed with his lucid advice, so I made an appointment, but I didn't go home. The next day my leg was even worse, and I was in wincing pain. It was all I could do to get out of my car. Something was clearly wrong, but I intended to push it as far as I could. I guess it was just a dumb guy thing. John cursed me for coming to work, and I told him I had an appointment the following day. That bought me some time, and he left me alone.

On Thursday morning I woke up with my leg on fire. It was huge and red and warm. I went to work before it was time for my appointment, probably just to aggravate John. I was having such difficulty walking that John was openly perturbed with me for even being there. "Go get your damn leg checked out now!" he demanded. He threatened to throw me over his shoulder and take me to the hospital himself. So I left work and headed to my doctor's office in Lunenburg.

I was in terrific pain when I arrived. I could barely walk. In a routine fashion, the nurse practitioner sat down in front of me and said, "Okay, let's have a look at your leg."

I stood up and dropped my pants. She looked up at me in a not-so-routine fashion and asked in a very serious tone, "Did you drive yourself here?" as if to say, "Please don't tell me you've been driving around like this." I told her I had, and she said matter-of-factly, "You need to be in a hospital." She told me she was calling an ambulance.

It was kind of an "oops" moment for me. I realized I'd pushed things a bit too far. Still, I asked her what the heck the need for an ambulance was. She told me I had a massive infection. Naturally, I knew I had an infection, but I'm sometimes someone who thinks if I ignore something long enough, it'll eventually go away. My entire upper leg from knee to hip was tomato-red and hot to the touch all the way from the front groin area around to the back, underneath my butt. I told her it hurt a lot.

Without trying too hard to mask her sarcasm, she exclaimed, "Ya think?!"

I told her that I was absolutely not leaving there in an ambulance. All I could see coming out of an ambulance ride was some type of huge co-payment, and I said, "Do you have any idea how expensive that is?"

Besides, my daughter had a chorus concert that evening, and I didn't intend to miss it. On top of that, I certainly wasn't going to leave my car a half an hour from my house and then have to figure out a way to go get it the next day. I think I might have been a little bit of a difficult patient that day.

She insisted. I insisted. I eventually limped out and left her no choice about the ambulance, but I agreed to go to the hospital. I assured her I would head directly to the emergency room. She told me to go down the street to Leominster Hospital. I continued with my defiance, however, and told her I was heading to Henry

Heywood Hospital, which was only a few minutes from my house in Gardner. She told me she'd call ahead. I guess I still didn't grasp the seriousness of my condition because I was genuinely surprised when I showed up at the Henry Heywood emergency room and a nurse met me at the door with a wheelchair and escorted me right in. No waiting. I remember asking the nurse, "What am I, some kind of celebrity?"

They took me in and assessed me. It appeared they were impressed with the size and the extent of my infection. It was quickly determined through testing that, in fact, I had contracted Lyme disease. But for obvious reasons, they were more concerned with the enormous infection, which was the clear and present danger, and the seriousness of it, which was the result of my own stubbornness and stupidity in not going to see a doctor in a timely fashion.

They hooked me up to fluids and medications and kept me all day and well into the night. I missed Bella's concert. By very late evening, though, they'd done all they could do. My condition evidently didn't warrant an admission, and they couldn't let me occupy a bed in the emergency room all night. They sent me home with a regimen of antibiotics and pain medicine. I went home and spent the night downstairs in my chair.

I'd been slowed down by a stupid, tiny tick and figured to be out of work for a little while. I was entirely unaware, though, that a chain of events was about to unfold that would not only slow me down further, and in much more dramatic fashion, but one that would change my life and touch the lives of many others. As unremarkable as the first domino was, it would set into motion a very remarkable sequence of events. In the morning, it was December 5, 2014.

It would be a day I will never forget.

FIVE

A WHIRLWIND COMES

In the morning I woke up in my chair to the sounds of Alethea getting the kids ready for school. When I began to stir, I was doing a bit of belly-aching, probably looking for a little sympathy and someone to bring me coffee. Jake, who was asleep on the couch in the other room instead of in his bedroom, which is in the basement, had been sick on and off since Thanksgiving. Alethea was having a difficult time rousing him.

What began as seemingly an average, every day cold with Jake, had persisted for several days. After the initial trip to the doctor's office a few days prior, there was no real reason for concern. It appeared to be a sinus issue. Soon he began to display different symptoms, however, as if it had developed into some type of chest cold, and he seemed uncomfortable. My wife, ever vigilant, took him back to his doctor where, the second time, an x-ray was taken. The image showed streaks on the lungs, and Jacob's doctor suspected what he referred to as a "walking pneumonia." They came home with the requisite antibiotics.

Over the next couple days, Jake appropriately acted under the weather, and he was a bit lethargic. He complained that it felt difficult to breathe. We still weren't overly concerned, though, as we felt that having breathing issues was rather consistent with having been diagnosed with pneumonia. We intended to let him rest and allow the antibiotics to do their work.

As I sat in my chair, I heard my wife continuing to try to wake him. Needing to move my body, feeling stiff after being in the chair all night, I got up, hobbled over to the living room, and told Jake something to the effect of, "Look, I can barely walk, and I'm headed to work (even though I'd already called out sick for the day). You need to try to get up, tough it out, and head to school. You've already missed enough classes. Once you get moving and get your blood flowing, you'll be fine." A teenager lying on the couch moaning and groaning about going to school isn't uncharted territory for any parent.

Apparently I was too wrapped up in my own discomfort to notice that he was genuinely sick. Alethea told me she thought something different was going on with his breathing. Perhaps the fact that he mumbled, "Dad, I can't breathe" should have activated my keen investigative skills. I looked closer, and sure enough, it did appear his breathing was labored, but it's difficult to tell when someone is lying down and wrapped up in a blanket. Not to mention, my powers of observation were likely not at peak performance at the time, based on my own condition.

Over my protests to give the antibiotics some more time to work, Alethea's motherly instincts took over. She took his temperature. It was nearly 103 degrees. She immediately declared she was taking him to see his doctor yet again. She told me to get him ready. I shook him a few times by the shoulder and scolded him again about missing school. I tried to encourage him to push himself to feel better. All I really wanted to do was get back in my chair. Truth be told, I was in such discomfort from my leg that I really wasn't paying much attention to anyone else around me.

"Okay, if you want to take him to the doctor, that's probably a good idea," I nonchalantly said to my wife.

I was truly not alarmed. A fever didn't faze me. We had five kids. Someone was always sick. Someone was always injured or dealing with something. Someone always had issues of some sort. It just is what it is. Over the years, we'd seen nearly every injury, malady, infection, virus, rash, bump, fever, bruise, and black eye imaginable. Alethea and I were seasoned MASH Unit parents.

My wife is a Supermom and can deal with anything, so oftentimes I took advantage of the luxury of being able to kick back and let her handle whatever it was. In this case, I was perfectly content to sit in my chair while she dealt with the issue of the day. Shamefully I can remember having the feeling that I couldn't wait until they got out the door. With the other kids being off to school, I'd have the house to myself. I looked forward to some peace and quiet, a coffee, and a painkiller. My intention was to simply sit all day and let my leg heal. My efforts to rouse Jacob and get him off the couch were short-lived. I wasn't feeling particularly useful, and Jacob wasn't responding to me. So I dragged myself back to my chair and figured I'd just let my wife handle it.

Things changed dramatically, however, when Alethea emerged from the living room a short while later with Jacob in tow. She had him propped up, standing in his underwear. She had the clothes she'd retrieved for him clutched in one hand while the other arm was straining to keep him balanced. She was supporting him like one would guide a wobbling drunk out of a bar.

He looked significantly worse upright than he had when he was lying on the couch. He was more than just unsteady in his gait. He couldn't stand. He was ashen. He looked as if he were assuredly going to topple over if Alethea so much as moved the wrong way. The look on her face said, "Please help me."

I jumped up and scooted across the floor like Quasimodo and guided Jake into the bathroom with her. I sat him down on the toilet while Alethea ran upstairs to get dressed. Then, like he was three years old, I tried to get him dressed. Something was wrong.

The lights were on, but no one was home.

Jake was mumbling. He couldn't communicate well at all. He was slurring his speech and moaning. He was struggling with simple motor skills. He couldn't stand or move without significant support. He reached with his arms to try to help me get him dressed, but it was like someone reaching around aimlessly while wearing a blindfold. His attempts were of little use and they worked against me.

I was trying to dress a limp and virtually unresponsive four-teen-year-old who weighed nearly one hundred fifty pounds. Then he started to vomit. It was most unfortunate that Alethea was al-ready upstairs by then because I generally don't do well with that. My stress level escalated a bit. With the labored breathing, the weakness and stumbling, the slurred speech, and now the vomiting, I couldn't figure out how I was going to get him dressed. Then, his nose let go.

Jake suffered from frequent and epic nosebleeds. Sometimes they went on for an hour or more. I'd seen him go through an en-tire box of tissues trying to quell a single nosebleed. I'd had the same issue as a kid, and it never went away until I eventually had the blood vessels in my nose cauterized in my mid-teens. It would appear I handed that undesirable gene down to my son. I don't know if it was related to what was going on in his body at the time, but of all the times for it to happen, Jake had the mother of all nosebleeds. It flowed like a faucet, and it didn't stop.

What a sight that must have been. We were jammed in our tiny first floor half-bathroom. I was basically high on pain pills and had the use of only one leg. Jake had no faculties about him what-soever, and I was trying to dress him while he flopped from one side to the other, dry heaving, and gagging. He was bleeding as if someone had cut him with a knife. We were covered in blood. I spun several feet of toilet paper off the roll to try to catch the blood while simultaneously trying to clean what I could. I held his head back and tried to apply pressure and talk him through it, but he just wasn't there.

He could do nothing to help himself. I tried to steady his head as it teetered from side to side as if he were falling off to sleep, while working to keep my own balance and trying to dress a young man who was taller than I and who was choking on the blood that was running down the back of his throat. He was coughing and inadvertently spitting it all over the place. When I bent down to try to get a boot onto his foot, I slipped in the bodily mess, smashed my head on the doorknob and got my leg wedged between the toilet and the vanity. Had it not been such a serious situation, I imagine if someone had seen this unfold, it could have easily been mistaken for a Monty Python skit. Alethea came downstairs and walked into a scene that, I have to imagine, looked like an axe murder had just taken place.

We finally got him squared away. Alethea cleaned up as best she could, and we got him out of the house and into the car. As testament to how selfish a person I can be, I felt relieved when they pulled out of the driveway and left—not because I didn't care that my son was obviously very sick, but rather in a way that I think a lot of husbands with superhero wives often think to themselves, "Damn, I'm glad she's got this!"

Even though Jacob was obviously sick, it hadn't yet crossed my mind that anything unusually serious was going on. Something was clearly wrong. That much was plain to see. But we'd seen it all before. There was no reason this would be any different. Among all our children, it seemed there wasn't an illness we hadn't experienced. We used to joke that we had to have amoxicillin on tap in our house.

After all, it wasn't as if he had cancer or anything. He hadn't been in an accident or broken any bones. He hadn't been shot, stabbed, or electrocuted. He wasn't poisoned. He hadn't fallen from a roof or a ladder or been struck by a car. It wasn't anything serious.

He was simply sick. He was going to the doctor, and he'd be home in an hour or so with the appropriate medicine. End of story.

With that as my thought process, I humped back into the house, cleaned up, changed my bloody clothes and plopped right back into my chair. My neighbor and close friend, Jason, stopped by a short time later with coffee and donuts. After the previous night in the hospital, and then the insane morning I'd just had, it was like someone showing up with a million dollars.

Jason and I were neighbors, friends, and partners in coaching. We routinely commiserated over life's trials and tribulations. He had three kids of his own, and he and I frequently exchanged our goofy family stories whenever a minor disaster occurred. I'd been texting him in my boredom from my hospital bed the night before, which prompted him to stop by. So we wisecracked about the tick situation. Jason is one of the most thoughtful people I know. He went out of his way to grab me something and come by to see me, knowing I'd been in the hospital and that I'd likely had a rough night. He had no idea what had transpired with my son only minutes before he arrived.

I showed him my leg like a battle scar, and we shared a few laughs. He commented that my leg looked as if it were going to explode and told me to take it easy. I mentioned to him that Jake had a tough morning and that Alethea had taken him to the doctor, and that I wasn't of much help. He told me I didn't look like I could be of much help to anyone. He made fun of me the way close friends do. It was a little payback for me having poked fun at him for a rather unfortunate tick incident he himself suffered some time before. I thanked him for the treats and he left. It's good to have friends and neighbors.

There I sat in peace and quiet with my dog, a coffee, and a donut. My leg hurt like hell, but at last everything was good. This was all part of the routine craziness of our home. I sank into my chair, and I'm willing to bet that soon I probably had all but forgotten Jake was sick. I dozed off in a rarely quiet and empty house. Then Alethea called.

She told me she was in an ambulance with Jacob on the way to UMass Memorial Hospital in Worcester. She was calm, as she usually is, and there was no alarm in her voice. The conversation was fleeting. She told me that when they arrived at the doctor's office, Jake looked even more awful than he had at home and the medical staff took him straight to the emergency room. She said she'd call back, and she hung up. I'm sure I didn't know what had just happened. I'm convinced that what she told me didn't register in my brain.

I don't remember how long it was before she called again to tell me what was going on, but there was a stretch of time. This time she was able to explain more. She told me they were now in the emergency room in Worcester and were headed to the Intensive Care Unit. Doctors were giving Jacob oxygen and trying to figure out what was wrong.

I'm a fairly smart guy, I think. I've been successful professionally. I like to think I'm pretty sharp and not unintelligent. But sometimes I think I'm capable of being utterly oblivious. It really didn't hit me that she was telling me that my boy needed intensive care, and what that actually meant. Despite the ambulance and the ICU, I was still in the mode of thinking that Jacob was just sick, that he was going to the doctor, that he'd get better and be home soon.

Alethea explained further, and I sensed more seriousness in her voice. When they walked into the doctor's office in Leominster Jacob's physical appearance was evidently so awful that medical staff immediately put a pulse oximeter on him right there at the receptionist's desk, without even going into an examination room. She said his oxygen was so low that it was immediately determined he needed to go directly to the emergency room. I'd been an EMT many years prior, and I knew that wasn't good. Oxygen saturation is vital. I immediately thought about his ashen appearance and labored breathing before he left the house.

From what I knew in my experience, normal oxygen saturation is between 95 and 100%. If it gets below 90%, you should see a doctor immediately because there's a problem. If it's below 80%, you're in danger of critical tissue and organ damage, and even failure if it's not soon corrected. If it's below 70%, generally, you're dying. Alethea told me that Jacob's oxygen level was in the sixties.

As I was processing what she'd just told me, Alethea told me they then put him in a wheelchair and whisked him down to the emergency room. Fortunately, Jacob's pediatrician's office was physically located within Leominster Hospital, and they wheeled him right over to the ER. It was immediately determined upon initial assessment that he needed to go to UMass Medical Center. She had to hang up again and said she'd call me back.

I tend to minimize things. I'd found that minimizing potentially stressful situations to a certain extent was an effective approach when one is in the military, law enforcement, corrections, or I should imagine, any emergency profession. In those arenas, you can't be the type who thinks the sky is falling every minute because you're always dealing with urgent or emergency situations. It is consistent, if not constant, crisis management in varying degrees. I'd served in several emergency disciplines over my adult life, beginning when I attended my first police academy at eighteen years old, fresh out of high school. I'd found that minimizing crises, whether done intentionally or out of habit, helps keep situations in perspective and enables one to maintain clarity and leadership ability. It always had for me.

Due to where my duties had taken me over the years, I'd witnessed and been involved in some spectacular, unbelievable, scary, crazy, wild, awful, amazing, and terrible things. During that time, due to necessity more than anything else, I'd developed the trait of being someone who was usually able to keep his head when others around me might be losing theirs. It wasn't because I was special by any stretch of the imagination. Like anyone else working in emergency professions, it was probably simply the result of having spent my career running toward danger and chaos, instead of away from it, as normal people do. It was my job.

During my career I had witnessed births and deaths. I'd seen shootings, stabbings, fights, and car wrecks. I'd witnessed hangings. I'd seen overdoses, horrific injuries, abuse, neglect, and rape. I'd been hit, punched, kicked, bitten, spat at, and assaulted with urine and feces. I'd had bullets and missiles fired at me. I had performed CPR and dressed wounds. I'd been involved in high-speed chases. I'd jumped from helicopters and rappelled buildings, cliffs, and mountainsides. I'd stood amidst the rubble of the World Trade Center. I'd been in the middle of a prison riot. I'd seen war. The point being that I wasn't an easily alarmed person.

I liked to think that having experienced such things had prepared me for virtually anything that might come my way. With the phone call from my wife, I'd just heard some seriously concerning news about my son, and the news was delivered to me by the person whom I loved more than any other. I resisted any urge to lose my mind. I calculatingly minimized the situation and I said "Okay." I sat in my chair and waited.

Alethea called me some time later to update me again, and it was then that my sense of urgency began to escalate. She told me the doctors at UMass were still doing their best to oxygenate Jacob while they were trying to figure out exactly what was wrong with him. I'd expected, or at least I'd hoped, that by that time, my wife was going to tell me the doctors had diagnosed what was wrong and were going to treat him, keep him for a day or two, and that the whole thing would ultimately boil down to a cool story about an ambulance ride for Jacob.

That wasn't the case. During subsequent calls, her tone gradually changed. Her frustration seemed to be mounting. She couldn't answer my questions. I, in turn, got frustrated with her and the lack of information I was getting. But she didn't know the answers because the doctors didn't know the answers.

I asked her, "What do you mean they don't know what's wrong with him? How do they not know what's wrong? What does that even mean? He's in an Intensive Care Unit, for crying out loud!"

In addition to my proclivity for downplaying the seriousness of any given situation, I have this unflattering character trait that when someone I love is hurt, or if I think that they'll be hurt, I get angry. I don't get angry at the person, certainly. I get angry at the situation. I get angry if I can't help them or if I can't prevent it. I don't know if this is common. I would imagine it happens to most problem solver types.

I'm the type of guy who sees a problem and goes right to work to try to fix it, even if I have no idea how to fix it, and even if I have no business trying to fix it in the first place. I do know that this has been the source of some consternation for my wife in the past, and it had made bad situations worse from time to time. I can't explain it. Perhaps it's a defense mechanism. Regardless, I couldn't fix anything that was going on. My son was in danger. He was now an hour away from me. My wife was getting scared. My leg was killing me. I had no answers. I was starting to get pissed.

I was obviously concerned, and certainly worried, but I don't think I was really alarmed yet. In fact, neither was Alethea, who at some point posted a rather benign comment on Facebook saying, in a very un-alarming fashion, that a weekend at the hospital with her boy hadn't been on her agenda, as if it were nothing more than an unfortunate inconvenience.

Alethea didn't want me driving to Worcester with my leg the way it was, coupled with the medication I'd been taking. She told me that if I needed to be there, she'd certainly let me know when that time came. I trusted her judgment. As the hours passed, though, Alethea's overall demeanor changed a little more with each call and each update.

Both of our mothers had gone to the hospital by this time. My oldest son had even swung by to bring Alethea a telephone charger as hers was in her van, which was now stranded in Leominster. Yet there I remained in my chair. There were still no meaningful answers as to what exactly was happening to my son. With each call, I began to feel more alarmed. The circumstances had begun to whittle away at my ability to remain calm. I couldn't sit and do nothing any longer.

It was time to go.

SIX

CONSUMED BY CRISIS

Jacob was awake when I arrived at the hospital. It seemed like ten or more medical staff members were working on him and around him, rushing in and out of the room. He had several IVs being administered, and he had a mask on his face to deliver oxygen. He still appeared lethargic, but I was able to talk to him, and he could respond. He had a nasal cannula underneath the mask, so he was receiving oxygen from two sources. He looked better than he had at home when I'd last seen him, likely due to the high amounts of supplemental oxygen he was now receiving.

We talked a bit. He was worried, but he was acting tough. We even shared a few jokes and laughs as I tried to make light of the situation, which is typical for me. I felt a great sense of relief speaking with him, and my alarm level went down considerably. My sense of reason told me the situation might not be as bad as I'd imagined. After all, he was conscious and speaking. That would prove to be a false sense of security.

Alethea had been there since the beginning, so she'd been observing everything and filled me in. I was now able to observe everything and speak with the medical staff to assess the situation for myself and put my problem-solving mechanisms to work. The disposition of the doctors left little room for interpretation, though. Despite the fact that I was able to sit there and converse with my son, his situation was serious.

The medical staff explained that, for all intents and purposes, Jake's lungs had collapsed. They weren't functioning. A collapsed lung occurs when there is air or fluid in the pleural space, the space between the wall of the chest and the lung itself. When that happens, the trapped air or fluid creates pressure against the lung, preventing it from expanding and thus preventing the patient from breathing. In Jacob's case, most of the air that was entering his lungs when he breathed was escaping into his chest cavity.

Not only was he not being properly oxygenated because oxygen wasn't reaching its intended destination, but because of where the air was going, it resulted in dangerous amounts of pressure in his chest cavity, which then caused other significant issues. The accumulating air created pressure on his other organs, and alarmingly, his heart. Still more alarmingly, the doctors didn't know why it was all happening. The problem solver in me asked matter-of-factly what they were going to do to fix it, fully expecting a concrete plan to be laid out before me. Surely this was routine for them. We were in an intensive care unit, after all. The tone in their voices and the looks on their faces made it clear, however, that there was no quick fix.

I was now most definitely alarmed. My frustration and anger increased. I knew my boy was in trouble. I was awkwardly moving about the room, barking in pain, and bumping into people and things as I only had the use of one leg. My right leg was like dead weight, and it was killing me. I had to hold on to the chair or the sink in the room to maintain my balance. All in all, things were awful.

Our lives would change dramatically over the next forty-eight hours. There was no longer any illusion that this was merely a minor illness and an unplanned and inconvenient hospital visit. It was no longer something to be made light of, minimized, or ignored. In short order, it became abundantly clear that our son was gravely ill. What we were dealing with was a matter of life and death.

As we processed all the information that we were being bombarded with, a flurry of frightening thoughts descended upon me. The totality of the situation began to come into view. Had Alethea taken my advice to just let the antibiotics work and had she not decided to take Jacob's temperature, which prompted her to take him to the doctor, it's entirely likely that she would have instead taken a shower and gotten herself ready for work and walked out the door. I would have been dead to the world, in all probability, dozed off in my chair. Jacob would have died lying on our own couch, only a few feet from me in the next room.

Or if Jacob had been sleeping in his bedroom in the basement, as he usually was, instead of being on the couch in plain view, Alethea would have tried to wake him up for school by hollering from the top of the cellar stairs, as she did every morning. If she hadn't actually seen what he looked like, she wouldn't have observed his physical appearance, which gave her so much concern. Again, she might not have taken his temperature. She might have simply let him stay home from school another day to sleep it off, in which case neither one of us would have known anything at all. Had I not inexplicably picked up a tick in December resulting in a nasty infection that kept me home, I would have left for work that morning and wouldn't have been there at all. We'd have found our son dead in his room.

To this day I have a difficult time even thinking about those things. Whatever prompted Jacob to sleep on the couch that night, which will never be known, saved his life.

⋙◆⋘

Doctors tried diligently, but nothing they did seemed to improve the situation. Jacob simply couldn't breathe. His body wasn't being sufficiently oxygenated, even with high levels of supplemental oxygen being pumped into him. His chest cavity was filled with air and fluid. Imaging and testing began to reflect widespread issues, including infection.

My years of serving in emergency professions, particularly my time as an emergency medical technician, provided me with a somewhat well-versed, albeit basic, knowledge of physiology and anatomy. I was aware that the gas exchange at the tissue level is what keeps a person alive from one breath to the next. If any part of the mechanisms and systems that deliver oxygen to the cells is in jeopardy, then life itself is in jeopardy. Oxygen was unable to be sufficiently delivered to the tissues of Jacob's body. When a person isn't breathing, they're dying. It's that simple. Our son was dying.

The ICU staff summoned numerous specialists from various disciplines. Pulmonary specialists and infectious disease doctors arrived to try to identify exactly what was attacking our son. They questioned Jacob at length to the point that he became frustrated and angry as they began to suspect that some type of recreational drug use may have caused the damage to his lungs (a reasonable suspicion, I thought, with a teenage patient). I never suspected drug use with Jacob, and I was confident in my ability to detect the signs of it if he were engaged in such activity. Still, Alethea and I immediately embarked on a widespread inquisition of Jake's siblings, our family, his friends, and even some of their parents, asking if anyone had any information or indication that Jake had been involved in any type of drug use. There was nothing.

For quite a while they ran through the gamut of things Jake could have possibly inhaled, either knowingly or unknowingly. They then began to suspect he may have inhaled something inadvertently that might not be drug-related. They hit Alethea and me with a barrage of questions as to possible toxins Jacob may have been exposed to in our home. They tested for every known substance, illness, bacteria, and virus. They collected blood and tissue samples and immediately sent them to specialists and testing facilities up and down the Eastern seaboard.

Doctors began to use the term ARDS (Acute Respiratory Distress Syndrome) in their diagnosis. ARDS is a state of respiratory failure with an alarmingly high mortality rate. Jake's lungs were under attack by what was now being referred to as a necrotizing pneumonia, which they suspected to be the cause of the ARDS. It was obliterating his lung tissue more and more by the hour.

The battle to keep an acceptable amount of oxygen in Jacob's blood remained constant. Among all the tests and the blood draws, the vital signs and the imaging, the numbers, pressures, and percentages, Jacob's oxygen saturation level became the Holy Grail. It kept fluctuating. It would hold steady for a while, but then it would invariably plummet, causing all available staff to race into action to adjust things in order to bring it back up, only to eventually see it fall again. Jacob went back and forth from looking extremely ill and in distress to being able to communicate and carry on something that resembled a conversation. He would go from being worried to being scared, to being angry, defiant, and impatient.

On Sunday he asked for Mom's phone so he could write something to his friends on Facebook. On December 7, 2014, from his hospital bed, unaware that he was standing at the precipice of the fight of his life, he would post the following on Facebook:

> Had a brutal night, but the day was fine. Slowly but surely getting better. Still trouble breathing, but I ain't going down without a fight. Thanks for all the prayers.

I had to admire his attitude and drive. His glass was half-full. I couldn't possibly give him the truth and tell him that there was nothing that was getting better.

On Sunday and into Monday, the growing frustration of the

medical staff began to look more like desperation. It started to shake me up. I was still waiting for the fix. When you're in crisis, you call a rescuer. But when the rescuer is in crisis, things aren't good. It wasn't a tenable situation. That's not to say that the people at UMass were anything less than competent and professional because they were marvelous. They worked on Jacob as if he were their own son. It was clear that the doctors and nurses were emptying their toolbox and trying everything they knew.

Having worked with and around medical professionals for a long time, I knew much of their language, and I was familiar (at least at a rudimentary level) with many situations and procedures. Knowing what I knew and hearing what I was hearing, I became more frightened. The atmosphere was tense. It looked as if the doctors, who I'd always regarded as (and who I always expect to be) superheroes, were exasperated and perplexed. They truly worked heroically to stabilize our son. But I grew more and more unsettled as I saw the urgency and, I think, the fear on their faces. My ability to maintain my cool was eroding ever more rapidly.

It was difficult at times to get a forum with the attending physician as he was so busy. When an appropriate moment presented itself, I posed one of those general, rhetorical questions that distressed people in hospitals often ask when they're trying to oversimplify things.

I asked, "You're going to fix him, right?"

The doctor I was speaking to looked me square in the face with a solemnity that frightened me, and all he said was, "I promise you, Mr. Nano, we're doing everything we can." That's about the worst thing you can hear. I held my wife and we prayed.

By Monday morning, getting near Jacob was almost impossible. So many staff members were constantly in and out, surrounding him. They were attaching machines, administering medicine, inserting tubes, and drawing blood. Medical debris was all over the place. It was a constant state of organized chaos. There was no down time. The efforts to keep him oxygenated and to deal with the multiple issues that were arising were virtually without pause.

Jacob grew less and less lucid. His words became fewer and farther between. Every chance we got, and any time there was an opening we could wedge ourselves into, one or both of us charged in to hold his hand and tell him we loved him. We did our best to reassure him, although I can imagine our own appearance was not exactly the most comforting for him.

He asked over and over again, "What's happening?"

I would turn away from him with tears in my eyes and try to gather myself, pretending I was looking at a monitor or something, trying to hide my own fear from him. I, myself, didn't know what was happening, so I certainly couldn't answer his questions as to what was happening. A more frustrating and helpless feeling I have never known.

At one point my wife pulled me aside and said, "I don't know if they can help him here. Maybe we should be in Boston." So many things were going on. There were so many thoughts and questions running through our minds. The scene became more and more tumultuous with each passing hour. The sights, the sounds, and the smells, combined with so many people speaking at the same time, and at varying volumes, were dizzying. I overheard many medical conversations in the room, down the hallway, and at the nurses' station, some of which clearly weren't meant for me to hear. Nothing sounded positive.

I picked out words and tried to decipher what was really going on and where exactly we were headed. I was confused. I was upset. I was aware that I needed to be an anchor for my wife, who was obviously upset as well. I don't know that I did such a good job in that regard. It was all coming crashing in on me. I thought I was a guy who could deal with anything and let nothing rattle me. But there was nothing I could do. We were going to lose our son. Our boy was going to die in front of us. I was rattled.

The next time I was able to corner the doctor, I asked him if they honestly thought they could help Jacob, or if we should take him to Boston (as if we were just going to throw him into the car and take off). The doctor said, "I promise you, if we can get him to Boston, we will." I remember thinking, *What do you mean if you can get him to Boston?*

By late morning on Monday, three days after Alethea brought Jake to his doctor's office, our entire lives, our focus, and all our priorities and concerns had completely changed. We were seventy-two hours into what would prove to be the crisis of our lives.

Whereas I always expect things to get better and for situations to improve, things were getting worse and quickly so. While we might have previously been downplaying things a bit to our family and friends, we were no longer doing so. We filled our families in on the gravity of the situation. Jacob was in serious trouble. Word traveled quickly that Jacob was in distress and that this was no ordinary illness or routine hospital visit. We were soon inundated with calls and messages.

Alethea and I are blessed beyond measure by the people we have in our lives. We both had family close by. Our parents, my brothers, her sisters, and all their spouses and children lived within an hour's radius of one another. We had an enormous support network of friends and family, which included our neighbors, our immediate and extended families, our sports families, our work families, and our church family.

We would need every single one of them.

SEVEN

AN ARMY ASSEMBLES

I always try to be a polite person. When someone leaves me a message, I always return their call. I think it's rude not to return calls or messages. It's a pet peeve of mine when someone doesn't do so. Despite the fact that any reasonable person wouldn't necessarily have expected me to reply to them, given the circumstances, I felt badly that I was unable to return all the calls and messages from my friends, and even from some of my family members who were inquiring about Jacob. My response to that situation inadvertently started a freight train rolling, the likes of which I'd never seen before. In a world of social media, the distress call went out quickly.

I used to poke fun at my wife for using Facebook. I didn't get it. I thought it was girly or that it was some kind of adolescent thing. From time to time, though, I found myself looking around on her account after she'd say, "Hey Hon, come take a look at this," and she'd show me something I thought was cool or interesting. When I began to periodically use her account, I ended up getting in contact with some people I hadn't spoken to in an awfully long time. I thought it was great. I found that I enjoyed it.

For a while I'd sneak onto her account when she was away from the computer, and I'd covertly surf on Facebook. If discovered, I'd still pretend I thought it was stupid, lest I be caught openly doing something girly. I eventually swallowed my pride, though, and made my own account. I ended up reconnecting with many old friends, particularly from my military days. I re-kindled friendships with people whom I otherwise would have never spoken with again. Some of them had been very impactful and important people in my life. I thought it was fantastic.

I found childhood friends who'd moved away, old high school chums, my brothers-in-arms from my Air Force days, the men I went to war with. There were so many neat things about it. On one occasion a guy I'd played some music with in high school contacted me and said he had something he wanted to send me. He sent me three songs I'd written when I was a young teenager, about the same age as Jacob. They were written, signed, and dated in my own handwriting on notebook paper. He'd had them in his possession for nearly thirty years. I think things like that are treasures.

On other occasions, I found that some folks with whom I served on the other side of the globe and hadn't spoken with in decades, now lived within an hour of me, yet I never knew it. There were some terrific reunions. Although I was in the closet for a while, in no time I became an open and unabashed Facebook user.

After people learned about Jacob's illness, it seemed my phone rang several times an hour. I found it frustrating. I couldn't possibly respond to them all while we were trying to deal with the situation. At the same time, I felt I couldn't ignore them. They were concerned. They were worried. If the shoe was on the other foot, I'd have certainly been calling them to offer whatever I possibly could. As I was never one to fail to answer messages, I grew a bit upset.

Alethea said, "Why don't you just post something on Facebook?" She was always the smart one.

Being unable to personally answer and update all the people who were trying to reach us to see what was going on with Jacob and if they could help in any way, I turned to Facebook. I posted a brief explanation of what had transpired. I apologized for not being able to return everyone's messages and texts promptly and individually, and I thanked them for their concern. I'm a very social person, but in some respects I'm also a very private person. I didn't feel comfortable airing something so personal in a public forum. I'm not ever one to talk about personal business, or any kind of business for that matter, in front of a crowd. Neither my wife nor I are the type of people who want or seek attention. I tend to move in the opposite direction of a crowd, and I generally take the road less traveled in any given situation. I much prefer to keep a low profile. In my mind the message was intended for my close family and dearest friends. Of course, the reality was that it was on the internet, so any intention I had of it being a closed conversation was an illusion.

Soon many, many dozens and, eventually, hundreds of people were responding and offering support and prayer for my young son. The texts, phone messages, and Facebook posts and messages were veritably endless. At first it was exceedingly awkward. Both my wife and I, though, soon found it to be energizing. It felt good to know that so many people cared about what happened to Jake and that they were praying for him, or at least they were rooting for him if they weren't the praying type.

People came by the hospital, sometimes just for a quick hug, knowing they couldn't meaningfully visit with us or with Jacob. They dropped off little bags for us with small necessities, the types of things you don't have time to think about when you're mired in a crisis. We were very thankful for things like toothbrushes, tissues, phone chargers, chewing gum, notebooks and pens, granola bars, crossword puzzles, coffees, and Advil. People's thoughtfulness was such a blessing. We wouldn't grasp the extent and the full scope of our support network for some time to come. We didn't know it at the time, but an army was assembling.

No matter what the medical staff did, Jake wasn't getting any better. Each hour's passing brought further frustration, more concern, more questions, and fewer answers. I kept imagining that at any minute someone was going to walk through the door and declare, "I know what the problem is," and then simply fix it. That person would never come.

The UMass Team constantly battled to get Jacob's oxygen saturation level above 80%. They would get there periodically, but they couldn't hold it. Jacob was coming in and out of lucidity in varying degrees. We continued to take every opportunity, when we felt we had a moment to talk to him, to tell him we loved him or to touch him. It was impossible to not be in the way, though. There were so many bodies moving about the room and so much activity and equipment that everyone was in the way. The frustration of the medical staff was palpable. They wanted to save Jacob as much as we wanted them to. We could see that their resources and their abilities were being taxed.

By Monday, Alethea and I hadn't really slept in nearly three days, other than the times when our bodies would shut down involuntarily and we'd catch a few minutes' rest in a chair. Jacob wasn't getting better. The attending physician pulled us aside late in the morning. He was holding some paperwork. He explained to us what we already knew: nothing was working and our son was in great peril. He had fought valiantly, but his lungs simply didn't work. His respiratory system was in failure, and his other systems were compensating and consequently suffering. He had major, systemic and life-threatening issues going on. The doctor told us they reached a point where they needed to sedate him, intubate him, and put him on a ventilator that would breathe for him. His urgency was unmistakable.

For reasons beyond my comprehension, though, I picked that time, of all times, to ask questions. I started hitting the doctor with multiple inquiries about what was happening to Jacob, what our options were, whether this was the best course of action, and whether or not it was absolutely necessary. I think I was scared that sedating him and ventilating him was putting him one step farther away from us when I wanted him to be closer. I suppose it was my way of stalling so I could have every minute with my son that I possibly could.

The doctor respectfully fielded my questions for a few moments but then abruptly interrupted me. He raised his voice and hardened his tone with authority. The actual words he used have escaped my memory, but the message was clear. We could either stand there talking about things, or we could do something. If we stood around talking about ventilating him instead of doing it, Jacob was going to die. It was a slap in the face that needed to happen. Sometimes people need to be slapped. I turned to Alethea, and she looked at me as if to tell me it was going to be alright. I took the paperwork and signed it.

The ICU Team clearly must have been preparing for the procedure already because, as soon as I consented, they rushed in like a finely tuned NASCAR pit crew and methodically went to work. We would only have a few moments with Jacob. Despite my state of turmoil, I became acutely aware of the possibility that this might be the last time I would ever speak with my son. While they prepared, Alethea and I held his hand, stroked his hair, and told him how much we love him.

Jacob was lucid enough to understand what was going on. He was scared. The fear in his eyes tore my heart from my chest. The image of his face as he repeatedly looked right in my eyes and asked me why this was happening to him is forever etched in my memory. I would have given my life without a second thought if it would've spared him his fear. The fear in my own heart was something I'd never experienced. He looked at me, crying, desperately reaching out for his father to help him, to do something, anything, to fix what was happening to him. There was nothing I could do to help my child in distress. A worse feeling than that, I would wager, a parent has never known. I'd never felt so helpless in all my life.

I tried to simplify everything, for myself as much as for Jacob. I told him they had to make him go to sleep so he could get better. Alethea did the same. We backed away, and in what seemed like seconds, he was gone. He went under and was silent. The sounds in the room, which were previously a consistent roar, quieted almost instantly to nothing more than the shuffling of feet, the beeping of monitors, and the rhythmic pulse of the ventilator, upon which my son's life was now balanced.

I looked at Jacob lying there in his sedated and unconsciousness state, machines streaming life into him. I was overcome by raw emotion. My seams came completely undone. I sobbed in agony. I cried like I'd never cried before. I could barely stand, and my wife didn't know what to do. All she could do was try to comfort me in her own sadness. She couldn't even hug me, though, because I sobbed with my entire body. I should have been the one holding her and telling her everything was going to be alright, but it was a force that couldn't be contained.

I like to think that if I had to experience it all over again, I'd somehow manage to push my own emotion aside and comfort my wife instead of losing my mind like an idiot. But of the many things I learned throughout Jacob's illness, one thing I learned was that matters of the heart cannot necessarily be controlled. I learned that control is one of the things in life that we trick ourselves into thinking is real when it's not.

I'm an emotional person, but I was never someone who really cried and certainly not in front of anyone. It's one of those privacy areas for me. I don't even like having a telephone conversation in front of other people, let alone crying. Before that day I could've counted on one hand the number of times in my adult life when I'd wept. Over the coming weeks, I would cry enough tears to last ten lifetimes.

Amid the chaos, our army had begun to circle the wagons to protect their own. People came. They came to the hospital and they came to our home. They came to hug us and to pray with us. They came to cry with us. Almost everyone who visited cried when they entered the room and laid eyes on Jacob. It wasn't easy to see someone they knew to be such a young, strong, and vibrant person in such a perilous and vulnerable state. I tried to give visitors a friendly warning to prepare themselves before they came in. When they told me that they intended to bring a child, perhaps one of Jake's friends, I advised against it. It was difficult enough for an adult to process. Several of our friends thanked me for that warning once they saw him.

Many people were lifting Jake up in prayer. I continued to receive messages by the dozens, offering support and asking for updates. I continued to make periodic posts on Facebook. My self-imposed obligation to respond to people continued, and to attempt to do so individually would have been impossible. Turning to social media became a brief respite from standing vigil over Jacob, a chance to step away from the actual situation and rest my heart for a few minutes at a time. It gave me an opportunity to clear my head, to briefly focus on doing something with my hands, and to simultaneously keep everyone in the loop.

I was never someone who thought they needed support for anything. I'd always been content dealing with whatever issues arose in life. In the past I had foolishly felt as if accepting help from people was a sign of a weakness of some sort. It wasn't long, though, before Alethea and I realized that we needed the help. We were in such a state of frailty and alarm that, at times, it felt like we needed help to just keep standing. Each person who offered their prayers and support was one more set of hands holding us up, keeping us from falling over. With each social media update, more and more souls enlisted in Jacob's Army, a term coined by his Uncle Eric, my brother.

Now that it was clear that this incident wasn't going to end that day, the next day, or any time soon, our families and neighbors began to organize managing our other children's activities and needs. Alethea and I weren't leaving Jacob's side. It became evident that we were in a marathon and not a sprint. I called the prison and told my boss I'd be out indefinitely.

There was no way I could go to work. I was very thankful that I'd rarely taken time off from work over the years and that, as a result, I had accumulated a significant amount of sick time. I don't know how I would have gone to work and dealt with the issues, the craziness, and the sheer ridiculousness of the daily prison routine while I was trying to deal with Jacob's situation. I would have been utterly useless there.

<hr />

Although being sedated and ventilated stabilized Jacob for the moment, he was in critical condition. Doctors didn't gain any ground in understanding what had happened to him with respect to exactly why his pneumonia had so viciously attacked his lung tissue if that, in fact, were even the case. The phrase "unknown etiology" would be repeated time and time again. The root cause of his condition was simply unknown.

It remained a constant challenge for the medical staff just to keep him in a state where he was critical but stable. It wasn't day to day. It was hour to hour. His body was sick. The state of his lungs and the physiological effect of what was consequently happening to the other systems in his body continually presented new issues for the doctors to deal with. Every time they were able to plug a hole in the proverbial dyke to stop a leak, two more holes would appear, and there were new leaks and new issues to deal with.

Due to the accumulating infection in his lungs and the ventilator not having the desired effects, even though it was on its highest settings, it became necessary to change Jacob's body position. He couldn't stay lying on his back, so they began a rotation of flipping him over.

For several hours at a time, he had to be on his stomach. A team would carefully and precisely manipulate all the necessary equipment and turn his limp and seemingly lifeless body over, and we'd spend lengthy periods unable to see his face. That was particularly hard on Alethea and me. Once they established how long he would be on his stomach, we'd watch the hands on the clock like kids in a classroom waiting for the bell to ring. As soon as the prescribed time was reached, we'd blurt out, "Turn him back over! Turn him over!" as if they didn't know it was time or they weren't paying attention. It was awful not seeing his face.

⋖⋗⋅◆⋅⋖⋗

Recognizing that we weren't home to shop for groceries or to cook for the other kids, our church family started a Meal Train through which people would sign up to bring our family a meal each evening. We'd communicate back and forth with the kids to let them know who was coming and when, so they'd be sure to answer the door.

Either Alethea or I would try to shoot home periodically, but we never left Jacob alone. Neither of us wanted to leave at all, and it always took some significant pushing from one of us to get the other one to break away for a couple hours to go home, freshen up, see the other children, and just get away from the hospital for a little while. Each time I left, I felt like I was racing to go as fast as I could so I could get back as soon as possible.

When I came home on Wednesday, our mailbox was literally full of notes and cards of love and encouragement. When I got settled at home, I sat and read the mail. It would be the first time of many when I would be overcome by the thoughtfulness, kindness, and awesomeness of people. The love expressed by so many would reduce me to tears over and over again in the coming days and weeks.

One aspect of the situation I had failed to appreciate until it was brought to my attention was Jacob's friends and classmates. Several days into the crisis, Heidi contacted me. Heidi was a dear friend of our family and had been our neighbor across the street for several years prior to her and her family moving to the next town over.

Not only was Heidi our friend, but she was also the nurse at Jacob's school. She served as Alethea's primary sounding board for all matters medical, as she obviously had a medical knowledge far greater than our own. She was a calming voice for Alethea, someone to hug, and more importantly, another mom who could share feelings and connect with my wife in ways that I, regrettably, could not. Heidi unwittingly became the first general in Jacob's Army.

Heidi reached out to me to let me know that the children at Jacob's school were concerned, something I simply hadn't considered to that point. She'd been fielding questions about Jacob daily from the students. All told, by that time, Jacob had been out of school almost entirely since Thanksgiving, when he first started getting sick. So, understandably, people noticed. In addition, I have to believe they'd been hearing from Nicholas, who I'm sure was talking amongst his own friends in the seventh grade about how sick Jake was. Heidi asked if there was an amount of information I was comfortable sharing with the student body.

At her request, I penned a message to Jacob's fellow students, which I tried to tailor toward middle schoolers so they could understand the situation but without frightening them. I sent it to Heidi who then presented it to the school principal. That day, I would later learn, the school faculty gathered the entire eighth grade in the auditorium and read my letter to them. Heidi would later tell me it was highly emotional as the kids learned that one of their own was in distress and in great need of prayer and support. Led by Jacob's closest friends and his brother Nicholas, the entire school would join the ranks of the rallying army.

This, in turn, resulted in the kids going home and telling their parents about the situation, ushering in a movement by an entire community. The communications to my family multiplied exponentially, and we became the recipients of love and support in such a fashion that I could hardly process it all.

I reached out to Jacob's baseball coach, David. A thoughtful and generous person, he is quick to help anyone who needs it in any way. His son, Lucas, was one of Jake's closest friends. I sent David a note to tell him that the information about Jacob was shared in school. I wanted to give him a heads up in case Lucas came home upset, and I filled him in on what was going on, which he had yet to learn.

David's wife, Sandy, is one of the sweetest people I know. Prior to Jacob moving to their school district, David and I were opposing coaches from different towns in Little League. But now Jacob played for him. As a result, Sandy and Alethea bonded as baseball moms watching their sons play together. We all became great friends. David and Sandy, without a second thought, immediately became generals in Jacob's Army and led the charge.

The next day I was on Facebook updating people on the events of the day and noticed a photo of Jacob attached to a fundraiser. Sandy, in her thoughtfulness, had launched a fundraiser for Jacob and our family to help us financially. In only hours, it raised over a thousand dollars. The donations poured in with notes of encouragement that tugged at the heart. I simply had no words for the kindness and the generosity.

Of the numerous profound aspects of Jacob's saga, one thing that impacted me to the point of being utterly overwhelmed on multiple occasions was just how awesome people are. People helping people; it's so simple, yet so profound. I'd always been fortunate enough to have always been able to be a giver. I'd been blessed enough in this life that I'd never really needed anything from anyone else. I'd never needed any help. The situation we found ourselves in with Jacob's illness, however, suddenly thrust me from the familiar and comfortable role of a giver to the unusual and, for me, the uncomfortable role of being a receiver.

I would be unable to count how many times over the years I was one of the many people throwing a twenty-dollar bill into whatever hat was going around, attending a fundraiser, providing a meal, or offering some other kind of assistance or support. Sometimes it was for people I knew; sometimes it wasn't. It was always the right thing to do. It was a given; it was comfortable; it felt good. But I never truly got it. I never stopped to really grasp the impact of people helping people.

At first, I found it very awkward. Someone would show up at my door with their children, carrying bags or boxes or containers of food. I wanted to say, "I don't need that. I don't need you to help me. Go and do that for someone who really needs help." I wasn't thinking it in an unappreciative way at all. I just figured there were people who really needed assistance, in my opinion, far more than we did.

I had worked from the time I was a young teenager. I'd never in my life been unemployed. I'd never had the misfortune of being injured and out of work. I'd never been unable to work or been unable to find a job, and I'd never been laid off. I'd earned every dollar I'd ever had. I had never been wealthy or even well off, but neither had I ever been broke, or down and out, or destitute. I always had shoes on my feet, medicine in the cabinet, ice in my glass, and food on my table. In the grand scheme of things, especially considering some of the things I'd seen in some of the places I'd traveled in the world, I recognized that I was rich beyond measure. I'd always been generally healthy. I had never been struck by any type of catastrophe or great calamity. I had never even felt the sting of death, as I hadn't lost anyone I was particularly close to. I'd never lost a close family member or dear friend, or anyone at all whom I deeply loved. For those reasons, it was difficult for me to see myself as someone needing help. I was blessed in life. It should be me who is helping others.

It wouldn't take long, though, for me to understand that now I did need the help. In short order I came to understand how much it really means when a brother helps a brother. With so many people in our community now being aware of Jacob's situation and driven by their desire to be of assistance, my family and I became the recipients of so much love and kindness that it brought us to our knees.

I began to see my brief trips home as a stop at a sort of spiritual and emotional gas station where I could collect myself, clean off the day's dirt, and refill my tank. Still, getting back to Jacob's side was the priority. I would do some speed-fathering with the other kids at home. I'd take some time, go over their schoolwork, try to explain to them what was going on with Jacob in terms they could grasp, try to convince them (and myself) that he wasn't going to die, address whatever issues they had, and jump back into the car to head back to Worcester. Each evening we prayed for Jake's recovery. My daughter, in particular, reminded me to slow down and pray with her when I was in too much of a hurry.

After I got back to the hospital on Wednesday evening, I shared with Alethea what all our people had been doing for us. Our army had formed and was at the ready. Then, that afternoon, another one of the generals showed up.

EIGHT

A BREATH OF LIFE

My church is a prayerful church. I learned much about prayer over the years through my pastor and fellow deacons. Still, I always felt that I never prayed enough. Prayer is a very personal thing. It seems to me that nothing could be more uniquely private than a person's individual relationship with God. I'd have to imagine that the dynamics of those relationships are as diverse as people are. For as often as I had prayed, however, and for my countless conversations with the Lord, He had never spoken back to me.

I'm someone who finds God in everything. When I'm in the forest or on the ocean, or any time I'm otherwise immersed in nature especially, I see God's mighty and delicate hand and His perfect design in everything from the trees, to the waves, to the creatures. Whether something good or bad happens to me, I look to the Lord for purpose and meaning.

Through good and bad, I strive to accept things as being the Lord's will, whether they're openly positive, or they bring with them misfortune or disappointment. Sometimes I'm more successful than others. I try to subscribe to the notion that life's individual victories, as well as its trials and challenges, whether minor or epic, all hold purpose.

Throughout my life I'd heard of people experiencing "God moments" when the Lord had spoken to them, or otherwise made His presence known, whether in subtle or magnificent ways. I couldn't claim to have ever felt His physical presence or that I ever heard Him directly speak to me. I'd certainly felt that the Lord had spoken to me indirectly on many occasions. For instance, I recognized what I interpreted to be the Lord nudging me in one direction or another, especially during times when I had a strong conviction about an important decision or problem. There were many times I felt like the Lord had shown me signs. Still, I'd never felt as if He'd actually spoken to me or that He was by my side in anything other than a figurative sense.

The tenth of December was a dark day. Our fear for Jacob's fate gripped us tightly. There were no good signs. There was no progress. He was getting worse throughout the day. As the hours passed, we latched onto what we thought were faint glimmers of hope or progress, only to see each one quickly dashed. We were scared.

In the afternoon Steve texted me to tell me he was on the way to the hospital. He told me he had another pastor from his church with him, and he asked my permission for them to come and pray over Jacob, and naturally I obliged. Steve met me with a hug. There was purpose in his step and a passion in his eyes. He proceeded to pray over Jacob as mightily as I had ever witnessed anyone pray. Steve's huge, resonant voice echoed throughout the entire intensive care unit. This was no soft or meek prayer of intercession on Jacob's behalf. Steve invoked the presence of the Holy Spirit with boldness and authority such as I had never seen.

Some nurses gathered in and around the room, and the attending physician stood in the doorway. When I noticed him, I approached him, somewhat apologetically, thinking that something might be wrong. I feared they needed to do something with Jacob, and that we were all in the way, or that we were disturbing the unit.

The doctor politely quieted me and said, "No. No. No. By all means, continue."

The medical team was invested in Jacob. It felt like they were more than just treating his condition. It felt as if in their hearts they were rooting for him as one of their own. They didn't like this mysterious illness coming into their house and threatening a child's life any more than we liked the fact that it happened to be our son's life that hung in the balance. The room was filled with energy.

Alethea's mother and her sister, Rachael, were in the room. All five of us joined together with hands and hearts, and we prayed with everything we had. Steve audaciously claimed Jacob as a child of Christ and called on the Holy Spirit to cast out his illness. He prayed with a joyful and commanding intensity.

That day, as they had been, the medical team was continuing to do all they could do to keep Jacob's oxygen saturation level as high as possible. Up until that point, they struggled to keep it in the eighties. Eighty percent is not good at all for a healthy person, and such a low level constitutes an emergency situation. But it seemed that was the benchmark for Jacob in his current state. Concern grew dramatically whenever it dipped below that mark. The longer his body endured oxygen deprivation, the more likely he would be to suffer lasting or permanent damage, if he survived at all. Each time the percentage fell into the seventies, the medical team sprang into action to take whatever measures were necessary to bring it back up, if only for a short period.

At the time we began praying, Jake's oxygen level was hovering around 82%. While we were praying, I heard some muffled conversation from the direction of the doorway to the point that it distracted me. I turned to see a look of amazement on the doctor's face. I followed his eyes, which were fixed on Jacob's monitor across the room. Jacob's oxygen level had suddenly increased from 82% to 92%. We continued to pray. Several minutes later it astonishingly climbed higher still to 97%.

Everyone was exhausted and emotional when the praying closed. I'd never been so overcome by prayer. Steve looked like he'd run a road race. He placed his hands on my shoulders, put his face in front of my face, and softly, but matter-of-factly, told me, "Jacob is healed." I remember the words, but I don't know if I really heard them at the time. I was a wreck. I was spent, both physically and emotionally. I was in a daze. I couldn't get a grip on what was occurring.

Jacob's oxygen level held steady in the nineties for several hours before it began to fall again. There was no apparent explanation for it. It wasn't as if physical restoration had occurred and his lungs were now functioning properly. They were still decimated. They were still under attack. He remained in very critical condition.

It was all painfully paradoxical for me. I was full of hope and faith, and yet I was frightened. Perhaps Jake's unexplained oxygen spike was coincidental or otherwise physiologically or medically explainable, but I had no issue believing that it was supernatural. Still, my child was dying. Although faith serves as a well from which to drink, it doesn't allow a person to escape the fallibility of their own human condition. I found that faith, as empowering as it is, doesn't necessarily eradicate fear or anguish.

There were numerous times when my heart was breaking, during which my faith, although ever-present, seemed to take a back seat to human emotion. Alethea and I strengthened one another. For each time that one of us felt weak, or if one of us wavered in our faith or allowed doubt or worry or fear to creep in, the other seemed to be armed with enough strength to carry us both. Any time we both felt weary, the ranks of Jacob's Army lifted us up. I have no doubt that the seventeen years we spent building our lives on love and faith is what prepared us to face this trial when it arrived.

To say that it took everything we had to get from one day to the next would be an understatement. To say that our faith made it easy would be a fantastic lie. Never had I experienced such colliding emotions. But whenever I started to beat myself up for the times when I felt as if my faith were waning, I reminded myself of Jesus' disciples. They walked with Jesus. They knew Him. They spoke with Him and ate with Him. They were His friends. They saw Him and touched Him. Yet even they had a difficult time believing at times, despite being in His physical presence and witnessing with their own eyes.

Thinking of that had always illustrated to me the frailty of being human. When Jacob was sick, there were strong days and weak days, peaceful days and angry days. Never, though, was there a day that wasn't marked at some point by mercy and grace, and at other points by emotion and imperfection. Although my faith was as strong as ever after we prayed with Steve, I was no less bound by fear.

What I believed was a holy presence had been a most powerful experience. I knew in my heart that something incredible was at work. When we prayed, it was as if the Holy Spirit were in the room with us and had breathed a healing breath into Jacob. Regardless of any possible explanation, or lack thereof, for several hours Jacob's body was filled with a breath of life.

That evening, as I was digesting the day's events and preparing for what the next day might bring, the significance of my friendship with Steve ran front and center in my mind. In the past, he and I had spoken often of the wonders of God and how He moves in our lives. Then, as if someone played a video for me to watch, I began to vividly recall several events that had occurred over the previous two years since I'd known him. I began to connect dots that I hadn't previously thought were necessarily connected in any way, and a picture came into view in my mind's eye. I saw the dominoes falling.

⊷◆⊶

I hadn't wanted to be transferred to the prison in Concord back in 2012. In fact, although I wanted to further my career and felt I would serve well in management, I was ambivalent about making the change. Despite being a promotion, it paid less than my previous position due to the fact that, as a manager, I would be on salary and consequently lose the overtime pay to which I was accustomed.

Coupled with the fact that I would need to spend twice as much on gas due to the longer commute, the financial concern wasn't negligible. That was to say nothing of the fact that I would also be leaving my comfort zone and learning an entirely new job in a new facility with a workforce with whom I was largely unfamiliar. I experienced quite a bit of trepidation in accepting the appointment. I prayed about those things, along with numerous other considerations, and ultimately I accepted the position.

In keeping with my usual way of thinking, I figured there must have been a reason I was being presented with the opportunity in the first place. I yielded to the notion that, if that was where the Lord wanted me to go, then I would go. I always tried to look at life's events as doors being opened. Sometimes it was easy to walk through a door, sometimes not so much. Sometimes what we find once we go through a doorway is welcome and expected and sometimes not. Sometimes we tend to brace our arms against the jambs and stand stiffly at the threshold. We race headlong through some doors, and others we need to be pushed through.

On that night, recounting the day's events, I became comfortable with the idea that I ended up in Concord some two years prior specifically to meet Steve so that Steve, in turn, could be with us that very night in Worcester calling on the Lord to breathe life into my dying son. I then realized that it wasn't the first time it seemed there was deeper meaning in Steve and I having become friends. It all started to come together for me.

Several months earlier, Steve, ever the pastor, came into my office and told me he'd been talking to one of our coworkers who'd been asking him questions about Jesus. According to Steve, he and Tony had been meeting together outside of work and talking. One day Steve asked me to speak with Tony. He felt Tony might benefit from talking to other folks as well and getting a potentially different perspective on some of his inquiries. When I eventually met up with Tony, I told him I'd heard he wanted to talk about some things. I knew him superficially, but we hadn't engaged in anything more than passing conversations.

Steve had told Tony I was a Christian and that I served as a deacon in my church. He told him he might want to ask me about some things that he was concerned with or some things that were troubling him. Almost as soon as I greeted him, Tony jumped right out and said, "Okay, so tell me this..." and he proceeded to pepper me with rapid-fire questions about God, the Bible, life, death, heaven, sin, and creation in such quick succession that I had no way of answering one question before I was hit with the next. He challenged me in the defensively inquisitive way of one who wishes to know about the Lord, but whose heart remains skeptical. He asked me as if I were some kind of authority when I considered myself to be anything but.

All I could do was provide the best answers I had, based upon my own experience and opinion, and on what the Bible had to say about it. We spoke many times. Tony asked questions daily, and this went on for some time.

Some weeks later, Steve approached me quietly, not in his normal animated fashion. He smiled gently and spoke softly when he said, "He came to the Lord." I knew exactly what he was talking about—Tony had accepted Christ.

At the time I remember having a feeling that there was purpose in my having gone to Concord and meeting Steve. I felt that the Lord was using us as instruments of some sort. We were insignificant people in an insignificant and unlikely place, yet I felt that something was stirring. Steve was a deeply spiritual man, so it made sense to me that the Lord would use Steve, wherever he was. But I wondered, as I had oftentimes in the past, why on earth the Lord would see fit to use me in any way or for anything at all.

Over the ensuing weeks, Tony would jubilantly tell us about all the new and exciting things that were happening in his life. He began to see his life, his career, and the world through an entirely different prism. A new passion existed in him that was infectious. Every time he told me about something new he discovered, I smiled and simply said, "I know, man. Ain't it great?" He began to see Jesus in everything.

Tony's teenage daughter, Julia, had been sick for nearly a decade. It was always very troubling to hear Tony speak about her condition. She suffered from Reflex Sympathetic Dystrophy, a particularly vicious and mysterious disease characterized by a dysfunction in the central nervous system that leaves its victim in unrelenting pain. It's a condition about which there are far more questions than there are answers. Julia suffered debilitating pain daily. She couldn't do the things other kids did. She was often immersed in pain throughout her body such that she couldn't walk or move. Tony shared with me that he frequently had to carry her up the stairs in the house or to the car. It was a constant battle for Tony and his wife to try to manage Julia's pain. As if that weren't enough, Julia had also developed a tumor in her brain and began to lose her eyesight.

Not long after Tony decided to follow Jesus, one evening he took Julia to Steve's church where hands were laid on her in the name of Jesus Christ for her to be healed of her awful affliction. On the way home, Julia told Tony that she experienced a strange sensation as if something in her head exploded.

Tony tells of being out in his yard the next day when he was approached by Julia. She told him with excitement that she felt no pain. For the first time in more than eight years, she was free of pain! To this day when Tony tells it, there are tears in his eyes when he recounts falling to the ground in praise and thankfulness.

A week later at Boston Children's Hospital, an MRI was performed to attempt to ascertain what was going on in Julia's body. The results were incredible. They indicated that Julia's tumor was gone. It wasn't smaller or different—it was gone! The tumor was gone. Her pain was gone. They would never return. She showed no further symptoms of RSD. She had been healed. There was no medical explanation. By all accounts, it was a miracle.

As I inventoried the chain of events and the falling dominoes, it all descended upon me in full force. I began to recall all the times Steve and I had talked with one another (and with other people) about the wonders of the Lord. I started to come to grips with Steve's enigmatic comment more than two years prior when we were still yet strangers, and he told me he'd been waiting for me.

I began to see that the tick hadn't been the first domino after all, as it pertained to the events surrounding my son's illness. As thoughts flooded my mind, I began to think that the reason I went to work at Concord was to meet Steve. Suddenly it was clear that it was no fluke that I felt the Lord's nudge when I prayed about accepting the position. I became convinced that whatever resulted in Steve being in Worcester on that day with his hands on my son and calling for his healing, had been in set in motion long before.

That day had been the longest yet. We were at a point where we knew we needed nothing short of a miracle. Despite our fear and weakness, we put all our faith in Jesus, the One who just so happened to be in the miracle business. Steve's declaration that Jacob was healed didn't eliminate my sadness and didn't eradicate my fear, but it bolstered my confidence, strengthened my hope, and emboldened my faith.

At the end of the day, I posted a photograph on Facebook for all the Jacob Watchers (as they had termed themselves). The photograph depicted me holding Jacob in his infant car seat when we were leaving the hospital two days after he was born. The caption declared with confidence that I had walked Jacob out of a hospital once before, and I intended to do it again.

The breath that was breathed into Jake oxygenated us all. The physical and spiritual rejuvenation was well placed because it would most certainly be needed. Jacob may have been declared healed, and our faith and resolve may have been fortified, but he most definitely didn't stand up and say he was ready to go home. In fact, things would get worse.

They would get much worse.

NINE

EULOGY FOR A CHILD

Jacob's oxygen levels returned to being alarmingly low. Things intensified over the next two days, and his overall situation drastically deteriorated. The hushed conversations among the medical staff weren't hopeful at all. I gathered indirectly from the things I heard that they expected Jacob to die. I kept hearing words and phrases like critical, respiratory failure, cardiac failure, unknown origin, survival, surgery, catastrophic, transplant, brain damage, oxygen deficit, and the like.

That's not to say that any doctor or nurse told me that the situation was hopeless. No one gave up hope. They intended to fight to the last. But in various areas of the intensive care unit, I picked up bits of candid conversations, a comment here or there, and the situation was painfully clear.

There were sporadic times throughout the days we were afforded an audience with one or more of the doctors when the situation allowed for a few quiet and focused moments to discuss things. I appreciated the honesty with which they communicated. They weren't hiding the fact that they didn't know why Jake was so sick. The chain of events was being pieced together, and it was clear that his lungs had been attacked by a particularly nasty pneumonia, but they simply didn't know why, and they didn't know how to fix it.

"But," I said, "people get pneumonia all the time. I don't understand."

They told us they had no idea why Jake's pneumonia caused such massive damage. The doctors unanimously told us that they'd never seen anything like it. That, in and of itself, was unnerving. I searched for quantifiable answers that might reconcile my logical thought process as to why we were in the situation we were in. I found none.

One doctor candidly told me, "I wish I knew what to say to you, Mr. Nano. What happened to Jake is one in a million. It's like winning the lottery. He just won the wrong kind of lottery."

As the hours passed, I juggled the nature of faith and healing with the acceptance of the real possibility that Jacob wasn't going to make it. When I leaned on my faith, I warned myself about the reality of the situation. Yet whenever I began to concede defeat, I fueled myself on the promise of faith. Whenever I stood triumphantly, I guarded against overconfidence. When I began to lose hope, I reminded myself of the wonder of miracles. I was embattled in the truest sense of the word.

I'd begun to think about death quite a bit. I didn't know how to process the death of someone I loved. Although it may sound contradictory, my faith and the unbelievable energy surrounding Jacob didn't alleviate my feeling of impending doom. A large part of me still felt he was going to die. I don't think the feeling was the result of insufficient faith so much as it was the result of being embroiled in a battle between the depths of my heart and the process of rationalization that was going through my mind.

Everybody dies. No one escapes death. Death doesn't discriminate. Good people die. Innocent people die. Young people die. Babies die. All kinds of people die for all kinds of reasons. Death is inescapably a part of life and an unavoidable characteristic of our human condition. Jacob was no different. He wasn't special. He was no different than any other patient in the hospital, many of whom would surely perish, and many of whom, no doubt, were the beneficiaries of prayer as he was. Ultimately, he would most certainly die. If not then, even if the healing was realized, he would still die one day. In a peculiar way I was preparing myself for his death, whether it came that day, the next day, or whether it was in a year, or in thirty years.

I obsess about things. At that point I began to obsess about death. What I felt was Jacob's imminent death weighed heavily on me. Outside of the obvious pain it would cause me and Alethea, it made my heart groan to think that Lisa would now lose a grandchild after already having lost her own son, Alethea's brother, Erik.

I couldn't stop thinking of the awful reality that when Jacob died, Alethea and her mom would then share the unspeakable grief, as mother and daughter, of both having tragically lost a child. I prayed for the Lord not to take him away from Alethea and Lisa.

Still, with the way things looked, I'd reasoned that perhaps it was simply Jacob's time. Although I knew I would have no possibility of understanding it, I could still find a way to accept it. I was never a "life's not fair" kind of guy. I wasn't disillusioned. I did not and would not pretend that I understood the Lord's plan for my son or for any of us. During many times in my life, I tried to make sense of the senseless and questioned God's motives. I found acceptance in the notion that it was impossible to understand such heavenly things when, in many cases, I couldn't even understand earthly things.

I wasn't traveling down a road of trying to understand why God would take my son from me. Rather, I was coming to grips with the idea that I wouldn't understand it at all. Sometimes I think that understanding that you can't understand something is the most clarity a person can hope to achieve. I didn't doubt it when Steve told me Jacob was healed by the Holy Spirit. I fully believed. But I had to leave room in my limited mind as to exactly how that healing would be manifested.

I surrendered any idea that I had any way to fathom the manner through which Jacob would be healed. I couldn't lean on my own understanding. I didn't know whether he was going to be healed in life or in death. I desperately wanted him to simply get up and walk out of the hospital, but I wondered if he would instead be healed in heaven. It was something I imagined but something I couldn't completely conceive. It was something that, even in my grief, gave me a sense of joy. I had an extremely difficult time trying sort those thoughts out.

After coming to terms with the idea of my son dying, through my sadness I found myself finding reasons to be thankful. I was thankful that I'd been afforded time to digest it all. I was thankful that Jacob wasn't taken from us suddenly, in an instant. Although I was gripped by the greatest heartache I'd ever known, I thanked God for the time I had with my son, as opposed to shaking my fist at Him for the time I wouldn't have with him.

Wearily driving home from Worcester to Gardner on Friday to spend some time with the other kids, shower, and change clothes, the prospect of Jacob dying wouldn't leave my mind. What initially looked like a positive day with a few small victories had taken several steps backward later in the day. Any ground that had been gained was quickly lost. Based on the looks of things that evening, to me Jacob's death appeared to be a foregone conclusion.

Perhaps the unrelenting ups and downs, along with the physical and mental fatigue that came with the passing of each hour, were taking their toll on me. I left Alethea at the hospital with a sinking feeling in my heart. I wasn't feeling positive in any way. There was a certain tenor to the interactions with medical staff. There was something about the looks on people's faces.

That night I felt he would die more than I had at any time to that point. I tried to imagine what it was going to be like when it actually happened. I remember thinking that the whole experience had really sucked to that point, and using my methodical thought process, I was trying to prepare myself for how much more that would be multiplied once he did die. Then, as if someone turned on a bright light, it suddenly dawned on me that there was going to be a funeral. The thought of a funeral hadn't yet crossed my mind.

My thoughts started spinning the way they always do when I begin to pick apart a problem. I was thinking about who I'd want to speak about Jake at his funeral. It didn't take long for me to decide that I didn't want anyone except me or Alethea speaking about him, and Alethea was out of the question. *After all,* I thought, *How could any mother be expected to have enough faculties about her to be able to speak after losing a young child?* So, clearly, the only logical choice was me. In a prideful and defiant manner, I thought to myself, *Damn straight, no one's going to speak about my son except me. He's my son.*

I reasoned to myself that, if I intended to speak about Jacob, I had better address the matter when I had my wits about me, rather than to reasonably think I could do so with anything resembling a clear head once he did pass away. I had the foresight to realize that if I was as upset as I was at that point in time while he was still alive and fighting, I expected I would be a puddle of a human being when the time actually came. I decided I had better do it then. So I went home and spent some time with Nicholas, Isabella, and Samuel. After I put them to bed for the night, I poured myself a rum and coke and gathered my thoughts. I worked up some courage, sat down at my desk, and did what no parent should ever have to do—I wrote my child's eulogy.

My eyes were flooded and swollen as the words came out of my heart and onto paper. In the past, I'd been to some tremendous funeral services that left me feeling like it was an excellent celebration of the deceased person's life. There had been times when I felt

I knew the person a little better when I left their funeral than I had before. I always thought that's what a funeral should be. I felt that a funeral shouldn't only honor the person's legacy, but it should leave people feeling happy and thankful to have known the deceased. Conversely, I'd also been to some funerals that were quite a bit less than impressive with respect to celebrating the departed and telling of that person's impact in the world for the blink of an eye they were here, or the legacy they may have left behind, or the things that made them special to the people who loved them. As I wrote, I wanted to make sure that people would have something to love, to smile about, and to hold onto when they thought about Jacob.

In truth, what I was writing was probably far more for me and my own heart than it was for anyone else who would hear it. It was one of the most difficult things I'd ever done. When I finished, I folded it nicely and placed it in an envelope in my desk. On the envelope I simply wrote "Funeral." It was the twelfth of December, my birthday. I was very sad but, at the same time, I felt peaceful.

In the morning any feeling of peace I had was quickly snatched up and snuffed out. The attending doctor approached Alethea and I with a sense of urgency and told us, "Jacob needs to go to Boston, and he needs to go now." Apparently, the opportunity they'd been waiting for had arrived. Despite their best efforts, they couldn't handle Jake any more in Worcester. He wasn't getting better, and they weren't equipped for what the necessary next steps would have to be if Jake were to survive. They felt there was a window of time in which they could possibly safely move him, and it was obvious that the doctor felt there wouldn't be another one.

He couldn't be transported by Life Flight because he required too much support equipment and too many staff members to be safely transported in a helicopter, to say nothing of the possible effects that altitude could have on his already ravaged lungs. The only option was the Boston Children's Hospital Mobile ICU transport. We felt better about the Mobile ICU with all its staff and equipment, but it required a larger window of time to accommodate than a helicopter would. At best it was a highly risky undertaking, and the tone of the conversation wasn't masked to indicate otherwise.

Alethea, her mom, and I consulted with the medical team who, as always, were transparent about what was going on. Jacob might not survive the transport. There was simply no choice though. It was gut-wrenching. If they transported Jake, he might not survive. But if he stayed in Worcester, he would most surely die.

By this time Jacob was being kept alive by an ever-growing multitude of machines, contraptions, and medicines. Everything would have to be delicately and precisely changed over to the appropriate gear that would fit in and be able to be utilized in the Mobile ICU. I can best describe the Mobile Intensive Care Unit as a super-ambulance. It basically appeared to be a firetruck, modified into an ambulance. It needed to have much more room than a typical ambulance to accommodate all the necessary equipment for an ICU patient on life support, as well as the necessary additional medical staff. We decided that my wife would ride in the ambulance with Jacob, that Lisa would follow, and that I would drive ahead and wait for them in Boston.

The preparation and the transfer took hours and was a harrowing process. Alethea's mom, who was undoubtedly one of the many generals in Jacob's Army (as were each of our parents), stood by Alethea's side as they painstakingly and methodically engaged in transferring Jacob to the mobile ICU bed. Jacob's vitals plummeted during the process, and he crashed. Lifesaving measures were undertaken. They stabilized him and carefully continued. As they were heading down the elevator to get Jacob into the vehicle, the attending physician accompanied them. He was a magnificent doctor. His concern and hope were genuine. Jacob's survival had become personal for him.

All told, from the time they began to prepare Jacob to the time he was ready to go, several hours passed. Alethea rode in the front of the ambulance because the medical crew needed to be in the back with Jacob. She couldn't see Jacob. She didn't know what was happening with him. They sped with lights and sirens, maneuvering headlong into the unforgiving Boston traffic in the giant vehicle. Alethea would recall that ride as being the most stressful and frightening experience of her life.

Boston was so close and yet so far away.

TEN

ZERO TO ZERO

I remember nothing of the drive to Boston. I don't remember leaving Worcester. I don't remember arriving at the hospital. I wasn't very familiar with driving in Boston and had never been to Children's Hospital for any reason. I don't know how I found it, or where I parked. I don't remember leaving my car and walking inside. I can only surmise that I followed signs to where I thought I needed to be. I didn't know where to go. I didn't know whom to see. No one was expecting me. All I knew was that my son was being transported there. In my emotional delirium, I'd taken off from Worcester in such a hurry that I failed to ask any informative or pertinent questions about what to do when I got there.

There I was, walking around looking for signs that might give me some indication of where I needed to go within the facility. It was eerily quiet, not filled with the teeming activity I expected to encounter in a major Boston hospital. Wherever it was that I ended up in the hospital, for whatever reason, there weren't very many people around.

A lovely lady, clearly a nurse, noticed my lost and shaken demeanor and asked if she could help me. No words would come out. I tried to speak, but I could only cry. Despite all that I cannot recall about that day, I will never forget the shattering feeling of having so much to say but being physically unable to utter a single word. Thoughts and questions tumbled through my mind. I wondered if they were already there. I wondered if he died during transport. I'd lost all sense of time and location.

Heavy, pooling tears blurred my vision and rolled off my cheeks. It was almost as if I could hear them crash to the ground. As hard as I tried, no words would form. Time stood still. The nurse held my shoulders as if to keep me from toppling over. I'm sure that any nurse at Boston Children's Hospital is accustomed to communicating with parents who are holding on to the edge of the earth by their fingernails, and I'm sure that's exactly what I looked like.

With extraordinary effort, and with the help of the nurse's calming touch and voice, I managed to finally say, "My boy." For a few moments, it was all I could say. After I eventually gathered myself and was capable of something that resembled coherent conversation, I muttered that my son should be there, somewhere. It was lost on me that I had blindly sped there, and that Jacob probably hadn't even left Worcester yet. The nurse took me around a few corners and guided me to an area of chairs within eyesight of what was evidently her workstation, and she offered me a seat. She brought me a ginger ale, took my information, and then returned to her desk, apparently to make some telephone calls. I fell fast asleep. As soon as I closed my eyes, it seemed, she gently woke me, looked at me soberly, placed her arm around me, and escorted me to the ICU.

Armed with the information she was apparently able to glean from whatever telephone calls she'd made, she told me that my son hadn't arrived yet, but that he'd be there shortly and would be admitted to the Medical/Surgical Intensive Care Unit. As it turned out, the transfer procedure was so intricate that it took nearly six hours for Jacob to be prepared, packaged, loaded, and transported from Worcester to Boston, a distance of only forty miles. I would later calculate that I'd been asleep in the chair for more than three hours. I never moved a muscle.

When I arrived at the intensive care unit, I was told to wait in what would be my son's room when he arrived. I stood there in awkward and uncomfortable anticipation of what was to come. I imagine I looked like a seventh-grade boy at his first school dance, standing in a corner trying to figure out what to do with his hands. Then I heard an announcement over the speaker system in the unit. Each time a new patient arrived, an ICU team number was announced and designated, and that team was informed they had an arriving patient, as well as which room the patient would be going to. The number of the room I was standing in was broadcast over the speakers. My heart pounded. Jacob had arrived.

As he came down the hall with his transport team, I hollered out, "Is he alive? Is he alive?" as I rushed toward him. A nurse politely restrained me and pushed me out of the way and told me he was alive. His newly assigned medical team sprang into action. They emerged from all directions and from out of every doorway. There seemed to be a dozen of them. Everyone went to work, and it was truly a marvel to watch. It was something I would love to be able to observe under other circumstances.

My being impressed with the efficiency and precision of the team was complicated by the fact that it happened to be my son's life which was at stake. The team operated as a well-oiled machine. The amount of activity was mesmerizing. People and equipment were flying all over the place. It seemed like there were fifty conversations going on simultaneously, yet everyone was in perfect synch.

A normally calm and collected type, I was reduced to wringing my hands. As we had become accustomed to, Alethea and I stood helplessly with our son's life in the hands of others. I had a million questions to ask, but no one to ask them to, as everyone was engaged in the flurry of activity. There are times when one interrupts and asks questions and there are times one knows enough to sit still and shut up. I don't know if it was more my state of shock or my recognition of that, but I remained quiet and still.

My state must have been obvious. I recall Alethea looking dazed or concussed, and I imagine I looked like I was going to explode. The team leader turned from the frenzied commotion surrounding Jacob, took my elbow, and sat me down. He could see I was barely holding on. He put his hand on my knee, looked me in the eye, and confidently told me, "You can only get nervous when I get nervous. And I don't get nervous." That was all. He slapped my knee and leapt back into action.

In "man language" what the doctor was saying to me was, "Brother, I know you're hanging on by a thread right now, and I know you're hurting. I know you're so worried about your son that you want to explode. But this is what we do, and we do it well. I'm gonna do everything in my power to take care of your son. So, try to rest easy, knowing we're working on your kid and will stop at nothing. If you see me get nervous, then maybe you can get a little nervous yourself, but don't count on it, because we can handle anything your boy throws at us. Everything's gonna be alright."

Of course, he didn't need to say all those words, but that's what I heard. Sometimes men can communicate eloquently using precious few words. It was exactly what I needed to hear. It got me through the next hour. From that point on, that's exactly how Alethea and I would live—one hour at a time.

They went to work once they had Jacob safely transferred and settled in. The conventional ventilator that was breathing for him in Worcester couldn't do the job of maintaining acceptable oxygen levels. By this time Jacob's lungs were all but obliterated. For all practicalities, he had no lung function. He was in complete respiratory failure. The medical team had to kick it up a notch to keep him alive. The settings on the conventional ventilator had been steadily escalated in Worcester until they were at their limits. As a result, the Boston team moved him from a conventional ventilator to an oscillating ventilator.

The oscillating ventilator didn't provide the smooth and rhythmic breaths that the conventional one did. The oscillator delivered constant and rapid breaths. It was loud, almost violent. While the conventional one delivered normal breaths somewhere around the rate of twenty breaths per minute, the oscillator delivered quick breaths at a rate of hundreds per minute. It was an intense treatment. It was difficult to watch. The rapid-fire breaths being pumped into him shook his entire body.

I wanted it to stop, but it was keeping him alive. From the onset of his sickness and during his stay in Worcester, and then in Boston, the pneumonia had done damage to Jacob's lungs which was nothing short of catastrophic, particularly in the lower lobes. Infection ran rampant throughout his body. His entire body was affected.

Small blister-like air sacs on his lungs called blebs had ruptured, basically riddling his lungs with holes. It was as if he'd been hit in the lungs with a shotgun blast. The air flowing through the ruptured blebs resulted in pockets of air and fluid being in spaces they shouldn't be, causing dangerous pressure. He developed conditions known as pneumopericardium and pneumomediastinum, resulting in pressure on his heart, his major vessels, his esophagus, and his trachea, all the way up and into his neck. He developed multiple bilateral pneumothoraxes and pleural effusions. Chest tubes had to be inserted on both sides of his chest to relieve the constant pressure inside his chest cavity.

He suffered widespread pulmonary edema and a condition called atelectasis, rendering his alveoli (the tiny air sacs in the lungs) all but useless. He developed issues with the ventricles of his heart. He had frequent fever that the medical staff had to continually fight off. He wasn't getting enough oxygen, and he had too much carbon dioxide, which was effectively poisoning him. He developed fluid in the abdominal cavity, which resulted in gall bladder, liver, and pancreas issues.

He was on broad spectrum antibiotics, sedation, paralytic, and other medications. He was losing body mass at an alarming rate. Jacob's disease was eating him alive. His arms and legs would eventually be reduced to skin and bones as if the muscles had wasted away. He developed bedsores, and his feet swelled. He had to wear pneumatic boots to help prevent heel ulcers and foot-drop from not using the muscles and tendons in his feet due to his comatose state. He was in bad shape, and it all happened so unbelievably fast.

Still, no one knew why. All they could do was to treat each disaster as it occurred. When they discontinued one medicine, they had to begin another. It seemed that as soon as they addressed or stabilized one area, another one became problematic. Hour by hour we stood and applauded little victories. But we were then quickly and consistently sat back down by new issues.

My wife's strength was remarkable. She hardly ever left Jacob's side. She couldn't bring herself to leave him. I would encourage her to take a break when one of us needed to go home, but more often than not, it ended up with her saying she simply couldn't do it. Sometimes I insisted and made her take a break, but she held vigil like nothing I'd ever seen before. She knew every medication and every treatment. She didn't miss a thing. She was on top of every machine and beep and blip, and she quickly mastered what each one of them meant.

She participated in almost everything with the nursing staff, even if it meant simply holding an IV bag. Her motherly instinct was a beautiful thing to behold. She neatly tucked away her agony in secret compartments so she could maintain clarity and resolve to serve her son. She was far stronger than I was. Her ability to nurture and to provide care, leaving her own needs behind, was unshakable. I needed to break away and lose my mind far more often than she did. I was comforted when I watched Alethea and the nursing team take care of my son. Her resilience was amazing. She is a very special person. One should hope to have someone like her taking care of them. She would have made a marvelous nurse.

My personal tug-of-war remained unrelenting. I rested in the belief that Jacob was being healed by powers beyond our grasp, but his prognosis was bleak, to say the least. While I understood the reality of what was occurring from a medical perspective, and while half of me was sure my son would perish, I dug deep with everything I had in order to hold on to both my earthly optimism and my heavenly faith.

I refused to concede defeat in the face of many moments when it appeared it was the only reasonable thing to do. I'd always approached life in that manner, and sometimes I tended to carry on striving for something long after it was obviously time to quit. Such an approach can be both motivating and admirable, but it can also be self-defeating. A fine line exists, I think, between stubborn resolve and foolish desperation. I've always been a fan of the underdog. I've always loved and embraced the idea of beating the odds. I always cheered for David over Goliath. I always welcomed a tough challenge. I taught my children that way. I coached baseball that way.

After any kid had been on one of my baseball teams for any length of time, he knew to never ask me what the score was while we were playing a baseball game. Any time during a game that any player, including my sons, asked me what the score was, there was only one answer: zero to zero.

I taught my kids to play like it was zero to zero, regardless of what situation they were in. It didn't matter if it was the top of the first inning or the bottom of the tenth in extra innings. It didn't matter if we were up by ten runs or down by ten runs. I taught them to approach every single play, every single pitch, like the score was zero to zero.

Sometimes in a close game, if we were playing at a field where there was no scoreboard, or when they simply weren't paying attention to how many runs had crossed the plate, invariably one of my players would ask me what the score was. Each time, the answer was the same. To me, there was no sense in looking at it any other way, because no matter what the current situation was, anything could happen. And it often did.

There were plenty of times in my life when I should have given up on something and conceded defeat. I always had a very hard time quitting. But for better or for worse, I've never been wired to give up. I'd fight and fight and fight for something, even when it seemed senseless.

I didn't do this in the spirit of being unable to accept defeat. My sons can attest to the fact that one of the things I taught them most frequently was, in fact, to learn to be able to accept defeat. I emphasized to my boys (and my other players as well) that it was crucial for them to be able to learn how to suffer losses with dignity. I guess I did it in the spirit of resilience.

After every game, before we lined up to shake hands with the other squad, I asked the boys what we do on the Phillies. They'd repeat back to me a phrase they heard often: "We win with grace and we lose with dignity." I never stood for rubbing it in someone's face when we won, and I didn't stand for failing to congratulate the opponent when we lost. This was always one of the parallels I drew between baseball and life.

I would tear into any of my players if I ever saw them act like a poor sport after they lost a game. I taught them that life is full of loss. I'd say to them, "You're gonna lose things, money, friends, girlfriends, jobs, family. How are you gonna deal with loss in life if you can't deal with it on a stupid baseball field?" I lectured them that a man's character is revealed in how he deals with losses, just as much, and perhaps even more so, as it is in his victories.

I could accept losing. I just couldn't accept quitting before the bell had rung, even if the odds were stacked heavily against me or all seemed hopeless. I approached everything in life with a "play until you hear the whistle" mentality. I certainly wasn't going to quit on my son. It helped that I had always been a glass half-full kind of guy. I usually had a knack of finding the good in any given situation.

I remember watching the movie *Soul Surfer* with Jacob. It's a story about a young surfer who lost an arm to a tiger shark, but who then triumphed over her loss to continue her passion of surfing. As we watched the movie, I asked Jacob if he thought he was someone who would be angry because he had lost an arm or someone who'd be thankful that he still had one left. I made it a point to always teach my children that there is good in any given situation if only they'd look for it. During Jacob's illness I spent a lot of time reminding myself of what I'd spent years teaching others.

I knew how sick he was. I knew the reality. I knew the odds. My acceptance of the situation, however, did little to ease its impact. I could say all day that I'd accepted it, but that never stopped the tears from flowing. It never took away the heartache. I could look at the glass as being half-full as much as I wanted, but that didn't take away an ounce of pain. I was full of hope and faith, yet at the same time I'd never been more heartbroken or sad. It choked me. It smothered me. I would exude strength and confidence for several hours and then invariably I'd hit a wall and find someplace private to lose it.

I had to dig deeper than I ever thought was possible to practice what I preached. It took all I had to keep my faith in Jacob's healing intact. It was like a punch in the gut every time I walked into his room and saw him lying there. Each time I walked into the room was like it was the first time.

I always thought I was tough and resilient. I wanted to be stronger, but it beat me up. I absolutely wouldn't quit though; and like any other parent who loved their kid, I never would. I felt like I was in a fight, and I kept getting knocked down. I'd pull myself up to standing, only to be punched and knocked down again. I had to find a way to keep getting back up, for myself, for my wife, and for my son.

With every passing hour, I told myself that the score was zero to zero.

ELEVEN

HEARTSONGS

It became all about time for the better part of the next two weeks. The days were long, and the nights were longer. The medicines, the treatments, and the machines had allowed Jacob to hold on, but he still wasn't getting better. There were positive moments but no major breakthroughs. The healing had been declared, but it had yet to arrive.

Just as they had in Worcester, the medical staff in Boston continuously fought to solve the riddles that Jacob's body was throwing at them. But as it was in Worcester, every step forward was met with two steps back. There were moments from time to time throughout the excruciating days that gave us slivers of hope. Every time the medical staff had any success, though, it ultimately only served to tease us that a turning point might have finally arrived and that he'd begin to improve. We were perpetually detoured by yet another new problem or complication whenever we thought we were heading down a positive road. With each new issue that arose, I learned a new multi-syllable medical term.

Whenever something positive occurred, I excitedly posted an uplifting social media update to keep Jacob's Army informed. Most of the time I didn't have the heart to follow the good news with the bad news, which invariably came next. It was almost as if I were worried about letting everyone else down. I began to feel a strange responsibility that somehow I was supposed to keep everyone else's spirits up.

Alethea and I became experts on vital signs. Jacob had more than twenty machines and IVs and various other medical contraptions attached to him. We spent hours monitoring them and interpreting numbers and alarms. The ICU nurses were magnificent, keeping us involved and informed. They asked for our help when it was possible for us to help, and they asked for our input and opinions. They asked about Jacob and the person he was. They talked to him all the time.

Alethea continued to help them take care of Jacob daily. She'd bathe him and wash his hair and comb it neatly as if he were headed out on a date. We provided an extra set of hands to the nurses when needed and when invited. It helped us keep involved and not feel like Jake was a lifeless lump lying in front of us. We knew all the names of our medical staff, and we interacted with them all day.

In a strange way being at Boston Children's was a double-edged sword. On the one hand (with absolutely no disrespect intended toward the tremendous people at UMass), it felt like we'd gone from the minor leagues to the majors. We felt as if there were no better place Jacob could be. On the other hand, we were at the end of the line. There was nowhere else to go. If they couldn't help Jacob at Children's, no one could. It was a sobering thought.

We tried to get home when we could for the other children, but neither one of us wanted to be the one to go home on any given day for fear that something significant would happen with Jacob while we were gone, and that we wouldn't be there for it. It was difficult for me to leave him at all, even for an hour, with the thought in the back of my mind that any time I saw him could very well be the last time I might see him alive.

111

With no end in sight and with us spending most of our time by Jacob's side, we felt as if we were neglecting the other kids, who were going through their own crises. Not only were they dealing with their own trauma, wondering if they'd ever see their brother again, but they must have sensed the distress that we were in, even though we tried diligently not to project it. Thankfully we had the army behind us.

One of us tried to get home at some point during each day, but that didn't always happen. Our folks and Alethea's sisters, Rachael and Rebecca, picked up the lion's share of the domestic duties at home for us. Several of our neighbors also checked in on the kids regularly and cheerfully offered any manner of assistance that was needed. I received calls and texts daily from people asking if any of the kids needed a ride anywhere or if dinner was taken care of in case the circumstances of the day or the Boston traffic kept one of us from being home at dinner time.

Scores of people came to Boston to visit us. Each time someone came, we warned them to prepare themselves. With rare exceptions, when they came into the room, they cried when they saw Jake's unresponsive body connected to the vast network of tubular circuitry, cords, and wires, along with the numerous machines and monitors. He was vibrating on his bed from the oscillator as if he were lying on top of a giant clothes dryer, his chest jumping in synchronous rhythm with the constant and resonant thumping of the machine. He was thin as a rail.

For several people it was the first time they'd seen Jake at all since he became ill, and it was easy to see that they were unprepared for the scope of just how sick he was. In some cases, we found ourselves comforting them when it was they who had come to comfort us. What we became accustomed to, and what was now normal for us, was shocking to them. On many occasions it ended up with us reassuring Jake's visitors that everything was going to be alright.

Every visitor was a blessing. They reminded us that we hadn't fallen off the map. We encouraged one another. Sometimes we'd laugh; sometimes we'd cry. Sometimes the timing of a visitor was impeccable and came exactly when one of us desperately needed a break, to go for a walk, or to go and try to eat something. The simple presence of another person was often good therapy. I have many friends with whom not a lot of words need to be spoken for us to be able to communicate. A hug, a look, and a nod were sometimes all that was necessary. Sometimes a few minutes' break from the stressful monotony was worth all the money in the world.

I talked to Jacob a lot as time passed by. I prayed with him, encouraged him, and told him jokes. I told him about the astounding support he had. Each time I came from home, I brought with me the latest pile of cards and read them to him to let him know how many people were pulling for him. I'd pull out my phone and read to him all the well wishes from social media posts. I wrote him letters. Sitting there feeling like I was doing nothing was torturous for me, so I always found ways to occupy the time.

I played his favorite music for him, and I would sing. Nearly every day I would pick Jacob's "song of the day" and post it on Facebook. I guess it was my way of reaching out to let everyone know that Alethea and I were by his side and that he wasn't alone, as if I needed to do that. I don't have a sweet singing voice, yet there I was singing to my son. I would hold his hand, and every so often while I was talking or praying or singing, I would feel a twitch, a little squeeze, something that told me he was still in there. Sometimes I could see his eyes move underneath his eyelids. My heart leapt every time it happened.

One huge concern that weighed heavily on us, in addition to whether he'd survive at all, was what he would be like when he woke up. I talked to him every chance I could, fearing that we'd never speak again, but also to keep his brain going. Jacob's body had suffered significant oxygen depletion for an extended period.

Although the doctors couldn't tell us that there would definitively be deficits when he awakened or to what extent they'd be, they prepared us to expect that likelihood.

There were many discussions about the effects of prolonged oxygen depletion on the human body. We wondered if he'd be able to speak, to walk, or to otherwise function as a normal teenager. Even if he were to survive this battle, we wondered if the son we knew would be gone forever. So, every time he squeezed my hand, or I sensed any type of movement or response to stimuli, I interpreted it as a positive sign.

I sang to him every day, hoping that somehow he was singing along with me. I hoped it was enjoyable for him. He loved music so much. I wondered if he had any level of consciousness. I figured he was probably bored to tears just lying here. I imagined that if it were me, and I was lying there paralyzed, I'd want someone to talk to me and play my favorite songs.

I sang songs while I sat at his side or as I shuffled around his room, inspecting equipment, monitoring statistics and machine settings, and organizing the growing amount of our possessions, which gave the appearance that we were moving in.

We did some Country. We did some Rock 'n Roll. I sang songs of hope, faith, strength, and endurance. I particularly love to sing hymns and songs of praise, and even though I concede that I'll never be a contestant on American Idol, I'm always singing something. Singing hymns, despite my sore lack of vocal talent, always provided me with peace. Singing to Jacob became therapeutic for me. It became one of the things that kept me connected with him, and it was something to take up a few minutes of time during the seemingly endless days and nights.

I would choose songs that expressed a theme for the day for us, or that reflected whatever message I was communicating to Jacob on any given day, or whatever was on my mind. Sometimes I found a song that spoke to a Bible verse I'd read. One particular song, and one of my very favorites, I sang day after day. It's called "Healing is Here" by the Christian band known as Deluge. It was an appropriate theme for me to have in my heart, and it took effort for me not to cry when I would sing it. I don't know if Jacob heard any of the music or the singing at all, but even if he didn't, it served as a sanctuary for me. I sang the words to him daily, telling him that his healing was here, that his freedom was here, and to look to the Lord as his Rock and his Healer.

I had a difficult enough time sleeping under normal conditions as a lifelong insomnia sufferer, but I had a particularly difficult time sleeping whenever I took the overnight shift at the hospital. My physical exhaustion and my racing mind didn't help. I would often take the night shift because it didn't bother me to stay up, and it provided Alethea some time at home in her own bed.

I enjoyed being there at night, as there was a bit more peace and solitude, and the unit wasn't quite as much of a buzzing hive of activity as it was during the daytime.

Apparently, my penchant for blessing the room with my less than perfect voice didn't go unnoticed. We largely had the same rotation of nurses caring for Jacob, but sometimes we'd have a new nurse.

Usually when one of our regular nurses was assigned to a different patient in another room for some reason, they would always find time to stop by to check on us. Often when we had a different nurse, one of the regular nurses would tell them at shift change, "You're in for a treat tonight. You're going to be serenaded by Mr. Nano."

One evening I was singing one of my favorite simple songs of faith called "You Are My All in All." It has a beautiful melody that, when it gets stuck in my head, typically lasts all day. It speaks of God being our strength when we are weak.

I was softly singing this song to Jacob in the dark, very late one night. I was seated beside him and holding his hand, a position I spent a great deal of time in. I felt two hands on my shoulders. They were small hands, and the touch was a motherly touch, clearly that of one of our nurses.

As I began a new verse and started to sing the song through again, a beautiful angelic voice joined in and sang along with me. Women have a unique ability, unlike most men I think, to be able to sing quietly and softly just as beautifully and with just as much feeling as when they sing openly and loudly. She sang ever so softly, yet at the same time it was as if it could be heard for miles.

For each verse I sang, she sang the chorus along with me in perfect harmony. It was tender, sweet, and prayerful. I laid my head down on Jacob's arm and fell asleep. I can scarcely imagine how difficult it is to work in a pediatric ICU day in and day out. I imagine pediatric nurses pray a lot. Many of our nurses wore crosses around their necks and were believers, but I would never know who it was who sang with me.

One day blended into the next. Whenever we needed a break from the full-time job of staying in tune with Jacob's daily routine, his advancements and his regressions, we found ways to keep busy. Alethea and I kept journals in notebooks through which we kept track of the date, what Jake's condition was, questions we wanted to ask the doctors, or anything else we found worthy of note.

I'd also taken to cataloging photos of Jacob and my other children to pass time. In the current day and age, with everyone having a camera on their cell phone, I think in general that we've lost some of the value and appreciation of actual photographs. I think back to when I had to make a special trip to the store to have the film developed, and I'd wait with anticipation for a day or two until I could go pick up the envelope and see the photos. I can recall what a thrill it was when they could process them in a couple hours, instead of days.

I had a thousand photos, some of which I'd never really taken the time to fully appreciate. I spent hours and hours, especially late at night, poring over shoeboxes full of family photographs. One evening I managed to construct a video montage of photographs of Jacob. I figured out how to attach music to it and make artistic transitions from one photo to the next.

I posted it online as an invitation for people to see the boy they were praying for as he grew through the years, and as a plea for them to continue to pray without ceasing until he came home. I usually took time each day, or at least every other day, to post something on Facebook for the Jacob Watchers. I was always amazed at all that had transpired since the previous time I'd been on Facebook. Jacob's Army grew and grew. I read every single comment and every prayer. Each one was like a glass of water to a parched throat.

At that time in my life, contrary to what I felt my true personality was, my heart was hardened and jaded in many ways. I'd developed something of a suspicious nature regarding people. Likely largely due to more than two decades spent working in prisons, I had an unhealthy expectation that people would lie, cheat, or steal (or worse) if given the opportunity. In some ways, although perhaps I didn't realize it, I'd lost a lot of faith in my fellow man. I can only surmise that it was the result of seeing the worst in people so frequently. I wasn't wired that way, though, and I hated it. So, every time I recognized that I'd been thinking that way, it made me sad.

When I witnessed the compassion for Jacob and the outpouring of love for our family, my heart became filled. People are just awesome. The people of Jacob's Army would change my life.

Twelve

Broken by Kindness

What my family was experiencing wasn't unique. Alethea and I were engaged in the same battle many had fought before us, and regrettably, many more will surely face—that of standing helplessly by while waiting for your child to live or die. We'd been derailed from our life's routine. We were in the middle of a terrifying storm, searching for any port or safe harbor. The regiments of Jacob's Army served as a lighthouse, and they did everything they could to make sure the light shined brightly.

Jacob's journey was more than an affirmation of faith. It was more than evidence of the power of prayer. It was also a showcase for the goodness that exists in the human heart and the magnificence of people driven to help others.

Despite having let a prevalent negativity creep into my heart over the years, Jacob's illness reminded me precisely of why I'd always looked for the good in any given situation—we are all in the same boat. And for someone who often thought he was totally self-sufficient or that he might like to be alone on a deserted island for a while, it taught me that sometimes it really does take a village.

Jacob's schoolmates responded to his plight in an incredible manner. They organized a school-wide event less than a week after my message had been read to them in the auditorium. The idea came from some of Jake's close chums and his younger brother, Nick. Since Jake's entire life was seemingly sports-related, they decided on a dodgeball tournament. They figured that they'd do something very Jake-like and run around like crazy people, throwing things at each other with wild abandon and laughing about it.

On the seventeenth of December, the entire school and much of the community converged on the school gymnasium and whooped it up Jacob-style. More than two hundred students and faculty signed up to play. Giant signs for Jacob adorned the hallways, communicating countless messages of love and support. There were enough faculty and students to form forty-five dodgeball teams. They played for hours. They shouted for Jake; they played for Jake; they prayed for Jake. They brought together an entire community for the sole purpose of lifting up one of their own.

Our friend Amy, another of Jake's friend's mothers, and a fellow baseball mom with Alethea, had t-shirts made with Jacob's number 21 on the back and the words Pray for Nano printed on the front. She sent one to the hospital for Jake. Alethea and I were both with Jake in Boston, so we didn't attend the event. In truth, I don't think either one of us could have handled such a social atmosphere at the time. Our mothers and my brother, Eric, went to represent us.

Sometime during that evening, Eric called me at Boston Children's with an excitement in his voice that I hadn't heard from him in many years. He was aware that I knew there was an event, but he told me I wasn't going to believe what was happening. He said he'd never seen anything like it. He sent a video to me on my phone. The students had filled the gymnasium bleachers with the force of love for their friend and classmate. They chanted and cheered and stomped their feet. It sounded like a rock concert. It was tremendous.

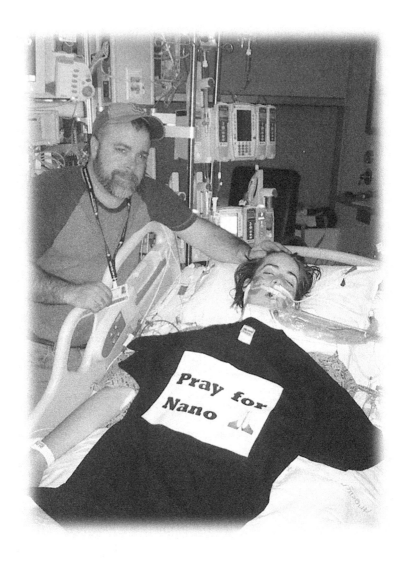

I played the video for Jacob as he lay in his bed. The cheering of all his classmates echoed throughout the intensive care unit. It choked me up. The nurses clapped and cheered. I asked a nurse to snap a photo of Jacob with his shirt so I could send it to Eric and the dodgeball teams could see him.

I later received telephone calls from a couple of newspaper reporters who asked me some questions about Jacob and about everything that was going on. Apparently, the community event had garnered their attention. Subsequently, two local papers ran a story on Jacob's ordeal. Jacob's Army, once again, spread even wider. The prayer, the love, the acts of the kindness, and the sheer awesomeness of people grew tenfold.

People lovingly came with meals every single day. They brought them to the house, and sometimes they even traveled to bring us a hot meal in Boston at the hospital, in case we'd been unable or unwilling to leave Jake's room. At first, I didn't properly know how to accept such generosity, but it didn't take long for me to feel and appreciate the love.

We each daily drove back and forth from Worcester and then from Boston sometimes more than once a day, depending on what was going on there and depending on what the other kids' needs were or any number of other considerations. There was no time to shop for groceries, to cook, or to bake. We were perpetually exhausted. I'd never had such a clear understanding of the meaning of the word weary. Eventually, when someone would show up at my door with something as simple as a lasagna and some bread, instead of feeling sheepish about it, I'd say, "Oh, thank God." Our people made sure my family always had enough to eat. Again, it was something so very simple and yet so wonderful.

The mailbox was full whenever I came home. It was typically overflowing with cards filled with prayer and encouragement, cash, gas cards to help us get back and forth to Boston, Dunkin Donuts cards to keep us caffeinated, and gift cards for whatever we might need. I thought back to the times I'd assisted others in need, and I always thought of my donations or helping hands to people as small and insignificant. Until then I'd never seen the full picture. I now felt the deep and personal impact of people's astounding generosity. What should have already been obvious to me became clear as I realized in dramatic fashion that no act of kindness is insignificant.

Jake's illness couldn't have come at a worse time for us from a financial perspective. Despite the fact that I had a good, steady job with a handsome salary, several circumstances over the previous several years left us in a position of being a paycheck-to-paycheck family. I'd even been in the unenviable position on a couple of occasions where I had to lower my head and take loans. We would have surely drowned without assistance during Jake's illness. Alethea had to leave her job as an early intervention teacher's aide to be by Jake's side, so we lost her income. Then, with the enormous cost of gas and parking, let alone the myriad other peripheral and surprise expenses, I'm quite sure I don't know what on earth we would have done without people's help. And the help came.

The dodgeball tournament alone, which I hadn't even realized was a fundraiser, raised over two thousand dollars. People from all over donated to help our family in many ways. We were humbled in the most genuine sense of the word. The campaign that Sandy set up on-line drew contributions from family, friends, and strangers across the country. It raised thousands of dollars. It absolutely blew us away that people would go out of their way and do such a thing for us. We were so deeply touched. Each day saw a new way in which people gave us a little piece of themselves.

Though it occurred decades before, I'd always remembered a conversation with one of my sergeants who often counseled me with advice when I was in the military. One time we were talking about friendship and trust, discussing our close friends and relationships, and he used a phrase that has stuck with me ever since.

We talked about friends, best friends, and "life friends." He told me that a life friend was someone you could call in the middle of the night if you were in trouble. You could wake them out of a sound sleep to ask for their help, and they wouldn't be upset or angry, and they wouldn't necessarily even wonder what happened. They would simply ask where you were and tell you how soon they could get there.

I'm blessed to be able to say that there are a number of people I can call in the middle of the night. It's something for which I'm very thankful. Ryan is one of my life friends. Even if we hadn't spoken in six months, if I called him, he'd be there. One evening I came home from the hospital after a long day with Jacob to find my dishwasher was broken. I knew that the odds of getting the kids, who were mostly home alone, to wash dishes by hand, were slim to none. In the grand scheme of things, it was a miniscule problem but an aggravating one nonetheless. It was something I just didn't have the time or the energy to deal with.

I called Ryan, as he was the first person I thought of who owned a pick-up truck, and also because he drives past my town on his way home from work. I asked if he'd do me a huge favor and run to the store on his way home from work, buy me a dishwasher, and drop it off at my house. I told him I would leave a blank check on the kitchen table for him and asked him to just fill in whatever amount the machine had cost him. I thought that asking for him to stop on his way home from work, pick out a dishwasher, buy it, load into his truck, and lug it into my house was a bit of an imposition, but I knew he wouldn't hesitate. That's just who he is. He let me know he'd take care of it. No problem.

The next time I got home from the hospital, I wearily pulled into the driveway, ready to grab the tool belt and wedge myself underneath the kitchen island for a couple hours to remove the old dishwasher and install the new one. When I got home, however, there was a new dishwasher alright. It was already installed. Ryan had gotten together with my father-in-law, Jay, another soul who's quick to help anyone in need in an instant. They'd removed the old machine and installed the new one. The blank check was still on the table. They both refused to take any money for it. I could only put my hands on my head in relief and thankfulness.

On another afternoon Ryan called me to ask if I was home. I was. He asked if the kids were home. I told him that a couple of them were there. He told me to hide them upstairs or something. So, I did. A short while later, Ryan pulled into my driveway and called me outside.

His car was full of carefully wrapped Christmas gifts. There were so many gifts that the car was so filled there wasn't enough room left over for a cat to have been able to fit into it. When I went out to the driveway, he jumped out and said, "Hurry up."

We unloaded the car and brought all the gifts, armful by armful, into the house and down to the basement. He and the members of his office, many whom were also friends of mine, wanted to make sure my kids didn't go without during the coming holiday. Ryan was a former member of my investigations team at the prison in Shirley. Like Ryan's new team, the remaining members of my old team at Shirley also joined forces even though I hadn't worked there in more than two years. They all made sure my family was well taken care of. I was speechless.

Our neighbors and friends, Carrie, Shannon, and Alyssa, all banded together and showed up with piles of gifts of their own. It was such a blessing to be on the receiving end of such kindness that Alethea and I could hardly find words. So often, Alethea and I would just hug and look at each other, and as was often the case, words weren't necessary. Each of us understood how overwhelmed the other was.

The doorbell rang another afternoon when I was home, and one of my co-workers, Kim, stood at my door with her husband and their daughter. They came in the door with so many wrapped

Christmas gifts they could hardly carry them. I tried to act digni-
fied and carry on a conversation, but I could barely maintain my
composure. Everyone was so worried that we wouldn't have time to
go Christmas shopping that they came to our home with more
gifts than I could even count. There was barely room enough in my
basement to move about. It looked like Santa's workshop. I had to
drape sheets over the piles to prevent the kids from seeing them.

My fellow Department of Correction employees, as they always do, rallied the troops when one of their own was in trouble or
in crisis. Fundraisers were held at the three prisons I'd worked at
over the years, and people showed up with heartfelt cards and en-
velopes full of cash. It got so that I had to prepare myself every
time there was a knock at the door because I knew I was going to
tear up in front of someone, an expression of emotion that had become the norm for me and one that was difficult to get used to. In
most cases I was their boss, so it was me who was supposed to be
looking out for them. I was humbled, embarrassed, deeply
thankful, and appreciative all at the same time. I'd never been the
recipient of such limitless generosity.

One evening an officer from the prison in Gardner, my home-
town, showed up at my door. He happened to be the father of the
little league boy who cried after our last game together. He gave
me a "bro hug" and said they'd heard about my boy, and he told me
the entire prison was pulling for him. He told me they managed to
pull together "a little something" for my family. He handed me an
envelope with over one thousand dollars in it. I'd never even
worked at that prison.

People from our neighborhood and our church showed up time
after time with armfuls of gifts for Jake and my other children. I'd
open the door, and they'd see my face, and they'd cry and hug me,
and I would cry and hug them. They just wanted to do something
to help. They showed up with food, with gifts, or sometimes just
for a hug or a prayer. In every conceivable way, they showed up.

When I wondered out loud why people were being so boundlessly kind to us, one friend told me that we were simply reaping what we'd sown. She explained that we'd been a blessing to others in many ways, on many occasions, and that the many kindnesses we'd provided to others over the years were simply being returned to us in our own time of need. It made sense, and it felt good to hear that, but it didn't make it any less overwhelming. It reminded me yet again that everything matters, and there indeed is purpose in whatever we do.

People would visit us at the hospital even if it was a time when they couldn't come in. Sometimes I'd hear from someone who came to visit, but I hadn't even known they were there because I'd fallen asleep. They told me they held Jake's hand and said a prayer and went on their way, not wanting to disturb whatever sleep I could manage. They would drive one hour, two hours or more through maddening Boston traffic in the dead of winter to see us, to hug us, or to pray with us. Coach David would frequently load Jacob's baseball buddies into his truck, buy a bunch of pizzas, and drive them all up to Boston to spend time around Jake. At the hospital and at our home, people continued to come.

Lee was a retired Correction Officer with whom I'd worked for many years when I was younger. He lived down the street from me, and he had a truck with a plow. The winter of 2014 and 2015 was relentless in New England. Record snowfall hit the area. We were clobbered by one nor'easter after another.

More than nine feet of snow fell in Boston and quite a bit more than that where we lived in north central Massachusetts. It seemed like it snowed nearly every day from December through February. I never shoveled once. Lee and others saw to it that our driveway was cleared and that we had easy access in and out if one of us needed to leave in a hurry. They came day and night. Sometimes they'd come several times a day. If a single flake of snow fell, someone came and plowed. There was never a time we were unable to get in or out of our driveway. When I was home, from inside the house I'd hear them plowing and try to throw on some boots and a coat in time to go out and express my gratitude, but they were usually gone before I could. They looked for nothing in return, even though they were deviating from their regular routes of paying customers. They just wanted to help.

One afternoon I was home and sitting at my computer paying bills, a mundane chore that doesn't go away just because you're facing a crisis. I pulled up the website to my children's orthodontist to pay the monthly bill for Jacob's braces which, like many other things, was overdue. I clicked all the buttons several times, but the site apparently wasn't working properly, and I was unable to pay the bill because it said that no account in my name existed. Frustrated after another long day, I dreaded spending time on the phone trying to straighten another issue out, but I called the office. I figured either the website was down, or the account had gone delinquent, and I'd have to explain that I'd been indisposed lately and then offer my apologies for being a deadbeat.

When I called, the receptionist told me I didn't have an account there. Before she was able to comment any further, almost angrily I told her I most assuredly did have an account there. I had been paying on it for over a year, and there was a balance of several thousand dollars as evidenced by the braces in my son's mouth. All I wanted to do was simply make a payment. She was finally able to speak when I took a break from my little tirade and stopped long enough to breathe. It turned out there was no malfunction. The website worked perfectly fine. Quietly and sweetly she said, "Mr. Nano, the doctor saw the newspaper article about your son. He figured you have enough to worry about right now. You no longer have an account with us."

I felt like someone had hit me in the head with a board. An uncomfortably familiar lump crawled up in my throat, a sensation I had become all too accustomed to, and choked my attempts at words. When I tried to speak to somehow express my gratitude, I couldn't control my emotions, and I burst out crying, completely overwhelmed at such a monumental gesture. It was several minutes before I regained my composure and could speak coherently. I believe in my heart that at that point I'd been utterly broken by kindness, if such a thing is possible.

I was overcome. I could have been knocked over with a feather. I wanted to thank her, but I couldn't speak. I was worried that she'd thought I hung up. She comforted me while I composed myself and said, "It's okay, Mr. Nano. Hang in there. We're all praying for Jacob. We're all with you. God bless you." There was this receptionist, someone whose name I didn't even know, on the other end of the phone trying to comfort me as I cried in her ear, telling me it was the least they could do.

It wasn't the least they could do. It wasn't the least anyone could do. It was the most they could do. I would be unable to count the number of times during Jacob's ordeal that Alethea and I were touched by or were completely and profoundly overwhelmed by kindness and generosity. I felt so thoroughly unworthy of such treatment that I didn't know what to do with myself.

For the rest of my days, I will cherish the awesomeness of human beings and the depth of the hearts of my fellow man that we experienced during those times. There were so many unbelievable and awesome things people did to make our terrible experience a little more bearable, many more than can be reflected here, none with any less significance or impact than another.

I'd never had such a feeling of community in my life. All we felt was love. We began to feel like the Lord was using the awfulness of Jacob's illness for good, and that somehow there was purpose in it. It was as if Jacob, in his comatose state, was somehow being used as a vessel for love, compassion, and kindness. He was unknowingly bringing people together in brotherhood and in prayer. People were at their best. Sun was shining through the darkness. People joined hands and they joined hearts. I began to see things differently than I had for a long, long time.

Throughout my adult life, my heart had been gradually broken one little piece at a time as I'd witnessed countless examples of despicable and abhorrent behavior. What I perceived to be an inherent awfulness in people, along with the things that I'd seen that one human being is capable of doing to another, had cast a shadow over my heart.

As someone who'd seen the worst and the darkest side of people on so many occasions, what we were experiencing restored my faith in humanity. I often thought of Romans 8:31 and wondered who or what could possibly stand against us in the face of such a fortified shield of love and prayer. For all that the people did, though—for all the love, the prayer, and the compassion, and for how solidly it buoyed us and gave us heart and hope, the insidious villain that held our boy hostage simply refused to loosen his grip.

The enemy would not go quietly.

Thirteen

LIGHTHOUSE

A week prior to Christmas, Jacob's medical team brought us the most distressing news we had yet to hear. In their exasperation, they informed us that it was nearing time for what would be, for all intents and purposes, a last-ditch effort to save our son. Jacob couldn't go on the way he was. Something had to give. As a result, we were introduced to the term ECMO. ECMO is an acronym for Extracorporeal Membrane Oxygenation. ECMO is used in instances of massive respiratory and cardiac failure.

In a healthy body, blood travels through the circulatory system and into the lungs, where it is oxygenated by the newly inspired air that enters the body with each breath. Once the exchange of carbon dioxide for new oxygen occurs, the blood is then pumped throughout the body to oxygenate the body's tissues through the incredible and life-sustaining processes of perfusion and diffusion.

When oxygenated blood can't be delivered throughout the body, due to the failure of either the respiratory or the circulatory systems, the body is dying. It's basic physiology. Without the exchange of oxygen and carbon dioxide, life ceases. The ECMO machine would artificially oxygenate Jacob's blood because his body was unable to do so.

As is the case with most last resorts, the procedure is very risky. Once hooked up to ECMO machine, the machine basically takes the place of the patient's heart and lungs. The patient's blood is actually pumped outside of their body. It travels through the tubes of the ECMO circuit, where it is artificially oxygenated, warmed, and then pumped back into the body where it can then travel through the circulatory system in order to oxygenate the tissues of the body and thereby sustain life. That such a thing is even possible is miraculous unto itself.

The good news was that there was still another tool in the tool box. The bad news was that, based upon our understanding and how it was explained to us, ECMO was the last tool they could use. At that time, Jacob had a very low chance of survival. I'd learned that when a patient is an ECMO candidate, they already have less than a ten percent chance of surviving. Once ECMO was initiated, his odds of survival in a best-case scenario would jump to somewhere around fifty percent if he lived through it. I profoundly struggled in keeping my chin up, trying to comfort my wife, and continuing to encourage Jacob deep in his slumber. Even if everything went perfectly, our son's existence in this world had come down to a coin flip.

———※◇※———

Back in 2012 I accepted a challenge from one of the officers on my investigations team at the prison in Shirley, Massachusetts, where I worked at the time. I joined a small group and registered to run a Tough Mudder race. For a guy my age and in the physical shape I was in at that time (which was basically round), the Tough Mudder would seem like an exercise in ridiculousness and futility. It's a race that is typically between ten to twelve miles long. It's full of challenging obstacles to test strength, endurance, and skill, and it's deliberately designed to be particularly difficult to see just how much heart each racer has. The last time I'd gone ten miles without the assistance of a car, boat, or plane, I was a youthful member of the United States Air Force Emergency Services Team. It was a lifetime ago.

Now I was forty-two years old. I was overweight, and my physical activity was, for the most part, limited to mowing the lawn and fishing, along with whatever exercise I got coaching Little League or otherwise chasing after my kids. There was no good reason for me to embark on this mission. I'm someone, however, who has a difficult time not accepting a challenge. Alethea wasn't initially thrilled when I told her about it, and I imagine she pictured me in a body cast when she asked if maybe my mind was thinking like a twenty-year-old while my body was anything but. As she always had, however, she supported my craziness and was my biggest fan. I knew it was going to be the most physically demanding thing I had done in many, many years, so I took the challenge seriously. I trained hard.

The street I lived on circled around and joined another street. That street then circled around again to rejoin my street at the other end, ultimately forming a large loop about a mile long that included a long, steep hill. I developed a love/hate relationship with that hill.

I started jogging to build my strength and stamina. Then I graduated to mixing in some sprints. After I gained some noticeable endurance, I began to stop every so often while I was running to do pushups and burpees and other calisthenics. After a while I developed a routine during which I would run with my music, and each time a song ended, I would drop to the ground wherever I was and knock out my exercises.

When I began to get stronger, I entered my self-proclaimed "Viking mode." I started to carry a log when I ran, and eventually I wore a back pack with half of a cinder block in it. I threw up in my neighbors' yards on several occasions and often had to leave my log somewhere along the route when I couldn't carry it any further. My back was cut and bruised from the cinder block, even though I wrapped it in a towel. I trained for the better part of five months. I ran whether there was rain, snow, or sleet. I was in a zone. When I could do ten laps around the loop, I knew I was ready. The day before race day, we all headed up to Vermont to Mount Snow, the venue for the 2012 New England Tough Mudder.

I was part of a team consisting of six guys from the prison and one of their wives. Ever the supportive wife, Alethea came too, and we stayed in a motel overnight. We drove by the mountain on the way to the motel and saw hundreds of racers, most of whom were young and fit, and who boasted something resembling a muscular physique. In the morning Alethea asked if I were sure I was going to do it. She knew better, but she had to ask anyway. I told her I hadn't done all that training for nothing. For better or for worse, it was happening.

I'd done some things in the past that had pushed my physical limits, particularly in the military. But that was when I was young, strong, and bulletproof. All things considered, the Mudder would ultimately prove to be the single most physically demanding thing I'd ever done. The course wound for more than ten miles up, down, and across the mountain. It was dotted with about fifteen or twenty daunting obstacles. I knew a stiff challenge was ahead of me, but truthfully I totally underestimated the mountain. It was far more challenging than I had anticipated.

The only thing I could really rely on to get me through the race was my experiences of having pushed myself, digging deep and having no fear, most of which came during my time in the military. During Operation Desert Storm I wore a desert camouflage bandana underneath my helmet. Of the few military mementos I still had in my possession, my bandana was one of them. It was more than twenty years old, tattered and faded. Prior to the race I tied it on, fully intent on channeling the young airman I once was.

Only minutes into the race, it was clear what I had gotten myself into. Once the gun went off, we commenced the very first leg of the race, which was an uphill run going straight up a ski trail and then back down another one. It became immediately apparent that having trained on a hill would prove to be invaluable. I felt as if I were spent after the very first segment of the race, and I still had 95% of the course yet to come. We hadn't even hit our first obstacle yet.

It didn't take long before I questioned what the heck I was doing. Not far into the race, one of my teammates would collapse with what we would later learn was a heart attack. He had to be evacuated from the mountain and taken to a hospital.

The rest of the team gathered for a conference to discuss whether we intended to abort the mission out of respect for him, or if we were going to press on. He encouraged us to finish the race for him as he was being tended to by the medics. The decision was swift and decisive. We had gone there to conquer the mountain, and that's what we intended to do.

The race was brutal. I won't pretend otherwise. It would have been a challenge even if I were still an athletic twenty-year-old. But at my age, with creaking joints and a bit overweight, it presented more than just a challenge. I nearly quit on several occasions. There were no fewer than a half-dozen times during the race when I almost convinced myself I couldn't go on another step.

I kept thinking to myself, *If I stop here, it's still a decent accomplishment. There's no shame in being realistic.* The obstacles were no joke. Many of them required teamwork to navigate. There is simply no way for a man to climb over a twelve-foot wall, for instance, without assistance. Then there was the mountain. The mountain was vicious and unforgiving. That race would have been difficult enough if it were a flat course, but being on a 3600 foot mountain made it a far sight more troublesome.

Every time we'd turn a corner on the course, we'd face yet another uphill climb. Up, down, and across the mountain's terrain we moved. There was one particularly steep climb that involved no running or jogging. It was so steep it basically had to be scaled on all fours. It was deep into the course. I stopped in the middle, halfway up, rolled over onto my back facing out over the magnificent view with the warm sun on my face, and that was it. I was all done. I'd made my decision. I'd already twisted both of my ankles by then and had tweaked a knee as well.

I was happy with what I'd accomplished. I decided in that moment that I was taking my ball and going home. I was done. I was disappointed in myself because I'd quit, but at the same time, I was happy with how far I'd made it. After resting a while, and with a sense of relief, I rolled back over to ease myself back down to the trail.

A good distance in front of me, though, was my teammate and close friend, Smitty. He was perched on a rock, some fifty feet above me in a squatted position looking right down at me. When we made eye contact, he must have been able to see my body language and the quit in my eyes. He wagged his finger at me and shook his head back and forth as if to say, "Not now. You're not quitting now. We've come too far. Let's go!" I was Smitty's boss and his team leader at work. I couldn't quit on him. Despite how badly I wanted to quit, I began to climb again, although I may have tossed some verbal unpleasantries in Smitty's direction.

The race was fraught with scrapes, bruises, cuts, cramps, and assorted other goodies. I even had to be rescued at one point. We came to an obstacle consisting of a rope suspended across a mountain lake. I have no idea how far the rope spanned across the water. It was a distance, though. If I had to guess, I'd say it was close to seventy-five feet across. The idea was to hang from the rope upside down with your feet looped over it, and to pull yourself across the rope and over the water, one hand over the other. Simple enough, it would seem. When it was my turn, I jumped onto the rope like I owned it. I swung my feet up for a firm grip and I pumped my fists, one over the other, as hard as I could, and I was flying across that rope. Or so I thought.

After a bit, I leaned my head back to see how much farther I had to go and saw that, much to my horror, I'd only moved a few feet. Suddenly I was exhausted. There was no way I was going to make it. Just then, as if it were on a timer waiting for the perfect moment, my right hamstring exploded in an agonizing cramp.

In response to the pain, I involuntarily released my grip on the rope in a reactionary manner as I reached for my leg and plunged into the icy water. It was only May, and we were on a mountaintop in northern New England. The water was nothing short of frigid. It sucked the breath out of me. Despite having grown up on the lake and being a very strong swimmer, I was in trouble. Tired, cramped, and wearing muddy clothing and shoes, I went down. When I came back up, I was in genuine distress. I couldn't believe it. Fortunately, the race people had the foresight to put rescuers in the water for the water obstacles. When I came up again, I saw one of the safety staff paddling around in a kayak. Our eyes met, and he saw what could have only been unmistakable desperation on my face and hollered, "I'm on my way, brother!" When he pulled up alongside, I grabbed the back of that kayak with everything I had, and he towed me to the safety of the shore on the other side.

My wife had obtained a map of the course and tried to follow us throughout the race as best she could by moving laterally across the trails, from one obstacle to another, so she might be able to catch us as we approached some of them and take photographs. She was able to navigate through the trails and was successful in arriving at several of them as we approached. The result was some really cool photos. She happened to be at that particular obstacle at the time of my mishap and snapped a photo of me being rescued. I look at that picture today and ask myself, "What the heck were you thinking, man?" Quite comically, the photo caught Smitty still hanging on the rope with a look of chagrin as I was conveniently towed past him to the other side while he still had to work his way across. Sometimes, you just need a little help.

I sat on the shore and watched my teammates finish the obstacle. Then we rallied as a group, and much like I had on the steep slope, I quit. This time it was definitely it. I was entirely spent, I was cramped, and now I had nearly drowned. But my guys prodded me onward. They refused to let me quit. My cramp subsided, and it was no small consideration that my wife was standing right there. I couldn't very well quit in front of my team and my bride. We raced on.

Some miles and several obstacles later, I was running (and I use the term running very loosely) through a section of mud that required significant effort to push through. My leg cramped again. This time it came with a fiery vengeance. I fell face-down in the mud, cursing like a sailor. A woman came upon me. She was twenty-something, perhaps in her early thirties at most. She told me she was a nurse and asked if she could help me. My sarcasm tends to grow as a situation worsens, and I told her she could help me if she had a helicopter to lift me off that stupid mountain.

She didn't have a helicopter. What she did have, however, was a banana and a salt packet that she magically produced from some mud-covered pocket or pouch. She asked if she could help my leg. I was writhing in pain. So, there I was, in a foot or more of mud, bleeding and dirty, slipping and sliding around with a total stranger who was trying to massage a mean cramp out of my leg. It was like we were engaged in a game of Twister while covered in lumpy pudding. She rubbed out my cramp as I poured the salt in my mouth and rifled the banana down my throat. Much to my amazement, in a few minutes I was on the move again.

I never looked back. When I crossed the finish line, Smitty was waiting for me. We embraced in a nasty, muddy, sweaty man-hug. It was the most tremendous feeling of accomplishment I'd felt in a long, long time. I was so excited I could hardly contain myself.

I had no business running that race in the first place. I certainly had no business finishing it. The very best and most physically fit racers finished in under a couple hours. It took me just under five hours. I don't know how I possibly crossed the finish line. What I do know is that I wasn't alone. Without the motivation, encouragement, and driving force of my friends, there was simply no way it could've been done. Without the unexpected and generous assistance of some strangers, I never would've finished. Without the presence of my wife and a personal disdain for quitting, I would've stopped less than half way through.

A photograph of me and my Mudder team sits on a book shelf in my office to this day, along with the ugly orange head band that each runner was rewarded with for completing the race. It stands as a perpetual reminder to me of what it takes to face seemingly insurmountable odds and still cross the finish line, even when you desperately want to quit.

With regard to Jacob's saga, the Mudder became a metaphor. After the race in 2012, Jake heard us talk about it. Somehow the obstacles were higher, and the water was deeper and colder in our stories. He saw all the photographs and the videos, and he thought it was just the coolest thing ever. He couldn't wait until he was old enough to register and run. He talked about it all the time.

So, as Jacob lay in his comatose state clinging to life, I talked to him about overcoming things. I talked to him about the Mudder. He was in his own race, and it was a lot tougher than the one I'd run. I spoke of the obstacles. I told him he wasn't alone and that family, friends, and strangers' love and prayer were helping him pick himself up and continue fighting and racing. I told him I wasn't going to let him quit because of the sweetness that would come with fighting with everything he had and then ultimately crossing the finish line.

Day after day as I sat by his side or in a chair a few feet from him, I wondered where he was. I wondered what he was seeing, what he was thinking. I wondered if he were dreaming, or if anyone else were with him. I like to think that he heard my words. I prayed that they served as a source of encouragement for him. I wanted to save him from his peril, to snatch him up from the danger, but there was no such option. Sometimes providing encouragement is all a father can do.

I told him how much I wanted to quit during my race, but that I didn't. I told him about obstacles I'd faced, not only during the Mudder, but in life in general. I shared some of my own personal storms with him. I told him to always look for the lighthouse because there's always one there, somewhere in the darkness. I joked with him that life would be no fun if it were easy and if we had no colorful stories to tell or scars to show. I told him I wouldn't leave his side. I encouraged him to keep running up the mountain. I advised him to attack every obstacle with everything he had.

I told him to keep swimming and that the Lord was in the kayak right alongside him, waiting for him to grab hold. I let him know that the shore was closer than he thought, and I counseled him to not be deceived by the apparent distance. I told him to stay faithful and strong. I told him to be brave and to face the giants. I told him that if he wanted to live, he just needed to keep fighting.

"Keep going, Jacob. Don't give up, son. Don't you quit. I know you're facing a raging storm, but don't you dare quit on me. Look for the lighthouse, son. Look for the lighthouse."

Fourteen

Blanket of Peace

The response to the need for prayer for Jacob was incredible. What began within our family and in our little church had now spread to the school, the community, and the far reaches of the internet. With all that was and always is going on in the world, I found it unbelievable that so many people pointedly took the time and offered their concern and passionate prayers for our son.

Our prayer family grew by the day. The army became legions. In addition to our family and friends, I was contacted by scores of people I'd never known who shared with me that, for whatever their personal reason, they felt compelled to pray for Jacob. While I naturally expected concern from those in our personal circles, I was completely taken aback by the investment of total strangers in Jacob's plight. We received communications and messages from so many people I couldn't begin to count them. Many of them began with, "You don't know me, but..."

I can only conclude that the elements of social media and the newspaper articles were responsible for the breadth of the interest in Jacob's case. Friends and family shared the story with their friends and families, and so on. Prayer requests multiplied exponentially. I received word from people that Jacob had been placed on prayer chains nationwide, and that entire church congregations were praying collectively for him all over the country and beyond. Even a church in Korea prayed daily for this young man in Massachusetts. I was never able to quite wrap my mind around the scope of the prayer and concern for our son. At the risk of overusing the word, it overwhelmed me.

Something amazing was undeniably at work. It couldn't be ignored. Decisive healing, however, would stubbornly refuse to reveal itself. My breath was still stolen every time I entered Jacob's room. No matter how spirited and rejuvenated I was, no matter how many days passed by, each time I returned to the hospital and walked into the room, it was still as if it were the first time. Each day felt like a new punch in the stomach from which I needed to recover so I could get my wind back.

There were so many ups and downs throughout Jacob's battle that there would be no way to number them. If ever there was something to be referred to as an emotional roller coaster, this was it. The support never diminished though, and I find it difficult to imagine what it would have been like without it. The people remained through thick and thin. Every time it seemed that I needed it, someone from somewhere would send me the exact message I needed to hear, precisely at the time it was needed. Thousands of hearts and hands constantly held us high. The prayers poured in. People prayed without ceasing.

The struggle for me between faith and understanding, between heaven and earth, and between heart and mind continued unrelenting. But I was never even close to being alone. I remarked to Alethea more than once how blessed I felt we were to have people. Together we wondered how anyone possibly manages such a life crisis if they don't have anyone to go through it with them and to share the burden.

Despite my many moments of weakness, my resolve somehow carried on, even in the face of defeat, even when I thought we were standing at the edge of total loss. I fully concede that the strength and resilience I was able to maintain was entirely derived from the Lord and the unwavering support of our army. There were times it seemed that death itself was standing in the room. I tried to ignore it, often with a seething anger. I had no intention to negotiate. When I felt weak, I was like a toddler placing my hands over my eyes telling death it couldn't see me. At other times I defiantly commanded death to get behind us and leave us alone. The myriad spiraling emotions tore at me with gnawing teeth.

For each time that my faith and confidence were unshakable, there was a time when I was sure Jake was going to die. For every hour I spent standing triumphant in Christ, armed with the promise of heavenly protection, the next hour I spent finding ways to accept the inevitable death of my boy. For each moment I spent holding my wife, reassuring her of divine providence and declaring her son's safety, I spent the next examining my own heart, digging for peace and understanding.

For each occasion when a doctor appeared to me as a heroic caped crusader, the next time they struck me as helpless and impotent. For each period during which I embraced acceptance, the next harbored conflict and uncertainty. For every time I excitedly informed Jacob's Army of any progress, I meekly peered over the horizon to the next expected problem and downward turn. For every victorious fist pump, I was rudely reminded of the absence of any semblance of true control.

I continued to talk, pray, and sing with Jacob through the nights. When I couldn't sit at his bedside any longer and I needed to move my body, I paced the room or sat in a dark corner. I occupied the blue-black hours deep in the nights by reading messages, prayers, and Bible passages, and by penning notes, poetry, and letters. Every hour that I successfully occupied felt like it brought me one step to closer to something, but to what, I didn't know.

On the nineteenth of December, it seemed as if the proverbial wall had been hit. Jacob had been in the hospital for just over two weeks, although it felt like two years, twelve days of which he'd been suspended in a comatose state. The prospect of the initiation of ECMO loomed like an ominous cloud. Nothing appeared positive. The atmosphere was heavy. Then came what appeared to be a baby step.

That day, based upon something they saw, doctors elected to transition him from the oscillating ventilator back to a conventional one to see if he tolerated it and to measure any possible progress in lung function. We interpreted it as a positive sign. Any positive sign equaled a positive day. I also interpreted it as being a daring move to see if there was any possibility we could avoid ECMO. The transition worked. The intense oscillator was replaced with the conventional ventilator and slow steady breaths now entered Jacob's body again. We tip-toed through the day with cautious optimism.

That evening I continued my therapeutic routine. I sat in a chair a few feet from Jacob in the crawling hours of the night. I watched him. I watched the numbers. I watched the sky outside. I fixed my eyes on the lights in the distance until they blurred and crossed my vision. I had to shake my head to snap them back. I hummed melodies. I prayed. I tapped my foot. I timed my own breaths with the ventilator so I could breathe with Jacob.

Calmness rolled over me. For the first time since the trial began, I felt as if my inner battles had ceased. I became enveloped in tranquility and enjoyed a sense of comfort that had previously eluded me. My hazy, semi-awake state changed into a crisp awareness. I became fresh and no longer exhausted. I was full of clarity and void of conflict. A transparent understanding fell upon me like a blanket. All doubt and fear left me. Jacob would live. Inexplicably, I somehow suddenly knew without any reservation in my heart that my son would survive.

The exquisite peace I experienced prompted me to write a

letter to Jacob right then and there. In the pre-dawn hours, wide awake and revitalized, I penned the following words to my son:

Dearest Jacob,

So many thoughts and emotions have flooded my heart over the past fifteen days since you were hospitalized. I have experienced a level of brokenness that I never thought was possible. These have been the most difficult days of my life.

Until last night my heart was in the depths of despair as I thought you would surely die. My soul was shattered at the thought of losing my son. God has granted me peace though, and now I know in my heart that you shall surely live. I have never felt the presence and the comfort of the Lord more clearly than I do right here and right now, in this hospital room, by your side.

We may never know exactly why this all happened to you, but I do know there was a purpose. The Lord has used you as an instrument to unite many, many hearts in hope, promise, prayer, and faith...

I don't know why God chose to use you in such a special and amazing way. What I do know is that I am now acutely aware of how impossibly much I love you. It has been revealed to me how much my heart is filled with unconditional love for my wife and all my children...I will be eternally grateful that God has chosen to heal you...You'll have to forgive me when you awaken if I hold you tight and don't let go.

All my love,
Dad

Unlike previous letters or notes, there was no hope in my words. There was no need for hope—instead, there was certainty. Jacob waking and returning to us was no longer an *if*, it was a *when*. His survival was no longer a wish or a possibility—it was a reality. The letter remains in the same notebook today, just as it was written on December 20, 2014 at 4:25 am.

That day we began to see a difference in Jacob's state. Minor advancements were made. Numbers and percentages began to look better. Conversations among medical staff, which had previously been dominated by a somber tone, began to sound different to us. The inflection in their voices changed during evaluations and during interpretations of tests and procedures. Among the medical staff, hope filled the room where caution, and even despair, had previously stood firm. Life took up a stance where death once stood. Where small victories had previously been immediately followed by groaning setbacks and ever present stumbling blocks, new obstacles no longer presented themselves.

We had become conditioned to treat any optimism with extreme caution, and so everyone except me was reluctant to rejoice just yet, but the day would indeed culminate in advancements without the accompanying regressions we had become so accustomed to. A growing anticipation was present. I decisively told every nurse and doctor who entered the room that Jacob would live. It was as if we were all watching a movie I'd already seen, and I knew the ending. It was impossible for me not to light up.

Spirits lifted. Smiles were seen. Conversations began to shed their foreboding undertones. The machines and the medications, much to everyone's still hesitant elation, looked as though they were working. It was the best day yet. Genuine hope from the medical staff was felt. They didn't need to put Jake back on the oscillating ventilator. They no longer spoke of ECMO. His lungs seemed to be holding, and they appeared to be positively responding.

The following day ushered in a sequence of events that would shake my soul.

Fifteen

The Gift

Early next morning I received a message from Carolyn, a friend and sister in Christ from my church family. She told me that she'd been in contact with a man she knew to be an incredible prayer warrior and a powerful intercessor. Carolyn told me she shared Jake's situation with him and asked for his prayer. She divulged that he later had some rather remarkable things to say about Jacob. I let her know she could feel free to share my contact information with him as I would be honored to speak with him, to say nothing of how intrigued I was.

That day produced even more dramatic change in Jacob's condition. His numbers improved. His functions increased. Doctors excitedly spoke of notable progress. The nature of the overall conversation surrounding Jacob went through a spectacular metamorphosis. Previously melancholy tones were noticeably upbeat. Not only was he holding steady, but doctors were able to actually decrease the oxygen and ventilator settings.

Jacob's right lung demonstrated so much unexpected improvement that they removed one of his chest tubes. The right pneumothorax showed signs that it had resolved, and it didn't reappear. It was real progress. He was still in critical condition, and far from being out of the woods from a medical perspective, but tangible and exciting forward progress had been achieved. People were clapping. Throughout the day we laughed, and we cried.

Amid all the positive happenings, the man Carolyn spoke of reached out and contacted me. He told me his name was Joel and that he lived in Texas. It was immediately clear to me that Joel was a deeply spiritual man. He proceeded to tell me that he was blessed with what he called the Gift of Tears. I didn't know what he was referring to. I didn't understand. I had never heard of the Gift of Tears.

Joel, a devout Catholic, told me that he first experienced this gift during a Sunday Mass. During the Consecration Prayer one Sunday, as he told the story, he began to weep uncontrollably. He shared with me that his initial reaction was that he was completely humiliated to be behaving in such a manner in public, especially in church. He didn't know what was occurring, but he said he was helpless to stop it.

The flowing tears, he said, weren't the result of his own sadness, pain, or even joy, as tears usually are. He described the tears as being the consequence of experiencing the purest love imaginable and of being in the presence of holiness and sanctity. As he described it, the tears were the human manifestation of the love of the Lord. They were inexplicable, and they were unstoppable. I began to feel physically weak as I digested what he was saying. What he was saying stopped me and forcefully gripped my heart. I recall my heart pounding in my chest.

Joel went on to share with me that some years prior, his own son was very ill. In fact, he was gravely ill and in a coma. Due to severe complications secondary to a rather common malady, Joel's son's lungs had filled with fluid and the fluid became infected. His blood had become toxic. His body was septic. He was terminal. The doctor told Joel that his boy would die and would likely survive only the weekend, three days at most. There was nothing that could be done.

Joel prayed over his boy. He prayed the Lord's Prayer, the Rosary, and every healing prayer from his prayer book. He prayed without ceasing for three straight days. On the third day, Joel described an energy building in the room that he referred to as "prickly electricity." He said that although only he and his son were present, the room felt crowded. At that time, he said he again experienced the Gift of Tears, just as he had in church. Soon, he said, he could pray no more and with a charge of what felt like an electric power flowing through him, he collapsed into a chair, utterly exhausted.

In the morning, he said he awoke to find his son wasn't dead even though his death had been forecast as a certainty. Phlebotomists came in for blood draws. They came back an hour later to repeat the tests. They then repeated the tests yet again, because the results from the first ones couldn't have been possible. His sickness had left him. The disease in his body, which had doomed him, was entirely eradicated. Over the next few days, Joel's son's body recovered, the lungs cleared and were restored, and he awoke from his coma. Upon his son waking, Joel described the doctor rushing into the room animatedly, right up into the lad's face and shouting, "You are alive because of a miracle! Do you understand me? A miracle!"

Something indescribable took hold of me as I absorbed it all. Joel's words penetrated me. I felt like I knew what he was going to tell me next. Joel then proceeded to tell me that he prayed for my son the day prior, after he received the request from Carolyn. He said that, once he began praying for Jacob, he again experienced the Gift of Tears. When he prayed for my son, Joel described being immersed in an indefinably intense spiritual experience during which he was in the very presence of the Holy Spirit. As during his previous experiences, he said his tears flowed from a love beyond description. He mysteriously told me that the veil between heaven and earth became very thin. He continued on and told me that

Jacob was loved by the Lord and that, in his sickness, Jacob was helping bring souls to God. I couldn't even process it, yet I could feel it. Everything in my heart leapt out. The hairs on my body stood up. My eyes flooded as multiple realizations descended upon me simultaneously.

To that point in Jacob's ordeal, long before I had ever heard from Joel, I held a deep conviction that something special was happening and that the Lord, for reasons far beyond my possible grasp, had been using Jacob as a vessel for love and compassion. My thoughts swiftly carried me back to UMass in Worcester where Jake's oxygen levels inexplicably elevated when Steve prayed so strongly as he declared Jacob healed by the Holy Spirit. Then I turned to the blanketing feeling of peace I felt when I wrote the letter to Jacob the morning before and a divine comfort and peace washed over me. I was shaking as I realized that, based on the timeline Joel was providing me, he'd been praying and experiencing the Gift of Tears the same day I was immersed in the unspeakably calming presence that told me Jacob would live, which was then followed by the incredible progress in his medical state.

Then I recalled a recent lunch Alethea and I tried to have together in a nearby food court. When we sat down to eat, I had begun to weep. I wasn't crying, per se, but tears fell from my eyes and wouldn't stop. There was no sound and I didn't even feel particularly or specifically upset. It was the strangest feeling I'd ever felt. Outside of the obvious overall situation, Alethea asked me what had made me so suddenly upset and I couldn't tell her. I just remember telling her, "I don't know. I can't stop crying." I remember looking down at my pants and seeing big wet spots on my thighs from the tears rolling off my face. I was embarrassed and even humiliated as we were in a food court in the middle of the city that was teeming with people at lunchtime. I tried to hide my face. I eventually left without eating. I didn't know what was going on. After what Joel told me, I felt I now knew.

All I could feel was love. All I could sense was God. I was speechless. But more than that, I was touched. I was touched emotionally, spiritually, and physically. When we prayed over Jacob in Worcester and Steve told me he was healed, it was a powerful thing. It was real. But there was something even more powerful now. I was overcome. I couldn't stop thanking God. I didn't know what to do with my emotion. I was totally overwhelmed with love and thankfulness to the point I felt I would fall over.

With a confidence unlike any I'd ever known, my faith blossomed, unencumbered by the weight of any doubt or fear whatsoever. Something outside of me and outside of everything I knew was happening. The peace I'd felt in the breaking hours of dawn in that hospital room the day prior, coupled with my interaction with Joel, was the most profoundly powerful experience of my life.

It is exceedingly difficult to articulate. I was certainly no biblical scholar and, truth be told, I never even regarded myself as a spiritually mature Christian. I was versed in the Holy Bible and had read a veritable library of Christian books, magazines, and other publications on a regular basis. I'd participated in countless Bible studies and attended numerous conferences. I'd frequently led my church congregation in prayer and also led many prayer meetings. So I was no stranger to speaking about or discussing prayer, the Lord, the Bible, or spiritual matters. I spoke the language.

But I simply had never been touched like this. Joel's words were entirely different. I'd never been so viscerally moved. What he was telling me stabbed at my heart and filled me with awe. It was as if his words were punching through me. I was struck with a powerful conviction that something unexplained and supernaturally wondrous was at hand.

My typical ability to minimize and downplay intense situations once again went completely out the window. Emotion overtook me. I was in the throes of a magnificent spiritual experience with a person who was telling me in the most compelling way possible that he had literally been in the presence of the Holy Spirit and that the very hand of God was on my dying son.

This man, who before that day I never knew existed, had shaken me to the core. Despite that I had precisely zero reason to trust him or hold anything he said in high regard, his words reduced me to a state of humility that I don't think I could even hope to adequately explain. He didn't tell me that Jacob *could* be healed or even that he *might* be healed. He didn't tell me to pray. He didn't advise me in the way fellow Christians typically comfort and encourage one another. The message I took from our communication was, "You may rest now. Jacob is healed."

I had spoken to the Lord countless times in my life but felt as if He'd never spoken back to me. I felt He now had.

In the weeks before that day, in my heart I had already laid my son at the foot of the Cross, so to speak. I'd left everything in God's hands. As previously described, I was extremely hopeful but also realistically prepared. I was ready for my son to live or to die. I was ready to accept either outcome, no matter how painful. I would continue, I resolved, to praise God in either event, despite the searing agony that would come with losing my boy. I knew that I couldn't possibly understand why the Lord would take him, if that ultimately ended up being the outcome, and there wasn't a shred of me that would have been happy about it. I hated it, but I'd come to peace with it.

Trusting in something you can't possibly comprehend must be the very essence of faith itself. Faith is truly a mystery. Although I had strong faith prior to Joel delivering his message to me, his message, coupled with the totality of the entire experience to that point, armed me with an unwavering confidence that there was nothing left to be hopeful for or concerned about. There was nothing further to worry about or to rue over. The score was no longer zero to zero. Victory was at hand.

After we laid hands on Jacob in Worcester, I had faith that he was healed, but I didn't know what it really meant or how it would play out. As far as I was now concerned, though, Jacob was touched by the healing hand of God, and all we needed to do was to wait. In what felt like authoritative confirmation of the shroud of peace that engulfed me the day prior, Jacob would most certainly live. Where I was previously burdened by what I expected to be Jacob's demise, I was now burdened by what lay ahead in what I knew would be his recovery.

When we prayed at the onset of his sickness, I *hoped* he would heal. When we prayed in Worcester, I *believed* he was healed. Now, with the Gift of Tears, I *knew* he was healed. There is an untouchable but exquisitely distinctive difference between believing something and knowing something. My blessed triumph was reflected in a message I sent to Carolyn later in the day after I recovered from my experience. It was simple, direct, and left no room for interpretation or ambiguity. It read, "Jacob will recover fully. And it will be a miracle of God."

All had been decided. The healing was here.

Sixteen

HEALING IS HERE

The coming days brought incredible and dramatic change. Jacob's condition improved by leaps and bounds. Though still critical, he was gaining ground and becoming more stable by the hour. Mechanical readings showed he was increasingly initiating and drawing his own breaths against the ventilator. Imaging showed the lungs clearing, lab tests improved, vital signs were stable, and ventilator settings and medications were able to be decreased. He was healing before our eyes. When a second chest tube was successfully removed, he achieved measurable expansion of his lungs, and no new pneumothoraxes resulted. His major systems were functioning at satisfactory levels. His lungs were holding.

Doctors and nurses consistently remarked on the level of healing they were witnessing. They used words like incredible, remarkable, and miraculous. Their astonishment was genuine. There was no way to mask it. The level of their amazement, although entirely thrilling, drove home the reality for me that they previously fully expected him to die. At one point a doctor told me and Alethea, "Someone is watching over your boy. People don't get any sicker than he was and live."

Not long before, it appeared as if he would be transitioned to

ECMO and that, with it, any reasonable hope for recovery would likely fade. We were headed in the opposite direction now. I caught doctors more than once standing with arms folded, shaking their heads as if they were marveling that all the medical rules had apparently been broken. One doctor told me as if she were trying to convince herself, "This…this is a miracle." She showed me the latest images of Jacob's lungs, and we compared them to imaging from the previous few days. She remarked that, had she not known any better, she would think the images were from two different patients.

The restoration of Jake's lungs was nothing short of astounding by medical standards. By Christmas Day, only four days later, they began to discuss weaning him from the sedatives and the ventilator. Given the suddenness of it all, and considering where we had recently been and how far we traveled in those four short days, it all seemed surreal. Instead of discussing burying our son, we were talking about waking him up.

I was frightened at the prospect of Jacob awakening. As I looked at him lying in his comatose state, his bodily functions having been governed by machines for weeks, I couldn't envision him springing to life when the ventilator was removed. I was so used to his silence. We'd become dependent on the machines as his lifeline. Thoughts of letting him fly on his own along with the various possible outcomes and consequences were quite unnerving.

As they reduced the amount of sedatives hour by hour, Jacob began to stir. After weeks of watching our son lie motionless, Alethea and I could detect even the slightest movement he made. Each one took our breath away. We picked up on every twitch of a finger, a foot, or an eye. He began to roll his head slowly from side to side. We would speak to him, and he'd respond with movement. His eyes would open periodically. When they did, I would jump to my feet so fast that I'd smash my knees on the bed rail.

The nurses and doctors spoke to him to explain what was

going on, in case he could hear them, so he could try to understand if he were able. The anticipation of what was to come was torturous, wondering whether he would be successfully removed from the vent or if he was going to be removed only to have to go right back on it. My biggest fear was getting a brief glimpse of life from him, only to have the door slammed shut, and then having him be placed back under sedation again.

I knew he would live. But I still didn't know what was ahead. It was wonderful and terrifying at the same time. We continued to pray. I had no idea what he could comprehend, if anything, but I coached him as much as I could and the best I knew how. I explained to him where he was and what had happened to him. After the medical team educated us as to what would take place, I told him what to expect. I told him that he was breathing by means of a ventilator, that he was getting better and that the doctors needed to turn it off so he could try to breathe on his own.

I told him it was going to be uncomfortable when they removed the tube from his throat. I kept telling him that Mom and I were right there beside him and that we wouldn't leave his side. I told him I loved him a hundred times. I told him to be brave and to conquer this obstacle so he could come back to us. It was only an obstacle, I said. It was just another wall in the Mudder that he needed to climb over.

On the morning of December 27, 2014, doctors announced that the moment of truth had arrived. They would remove Jacob from the ventilator to see how he responded. They repeatedly cautioned us to keep things in perspective. They were optimistic but very cautiously so. There was a likelihood that he would need to be vented again. They prepared us.

When Jake played football for the Panthers the year they won the state title, they had a game day tradition. At each home game, prior to taking the field, the song "Kickstart My Heart" by the heavy metal band Motley Crue was cranked out over the loudspeaker system. It's a raucous, adrenaline-pumping tune that lives up to its title. The football team would build up its energy during the opening chords and then when the guitar riff would break in along with the pounding drums, they'd charge the field like they were running into medieval battle, where they would invariably vanquish the enemy.

I placed my phone next to Jake, opened my playlists, found the song, and cranked it up. In what I imagine might have been a first for the Med/Surg ICU at Boston Children's Hospital, Motley Crue rocked the unit. I don't know if Jake could hear it at all, but it got me fired up like I hadn't been in a long, long time. It's virtually impossible to listen to that song and not move your body. Nurses played air guitar and pumped their fists. It was go time.

The brief escape that Motley Crue provided us was short-lived. The drums and guitars were soon replaced by the deadly serious din of a precision medical team preparing to bring my boy from beyond consciousness to being back among the living. Alethea prayed. I paced. I occupied my hands with picking up specks on the floor that no one would ever notice. I randomly adjusted a chair, a hanging coat, or a picture on a wall that didn't need adjusting. I did anything to occupy myself if only to fill the space of even a few seconds. I remember opening random drawers and organizing medical supplies.

Jacob began to stir more and more by the minute. Soon he was awake. He was able to communicate in the most rudimentary ways possible. He was trying to move and shed the medicinal shackles that were binding him. He was clawing his way out of unconsciousness. Although they peeled back the sedatives enough to rouse him from his comatose state, he still had enough drugs in him to knock out a rhino. But he was unmistakably in there. Jake was awake.

Nurses spoke to him in that loud, deliberate manner when they overly enunciate each word they're saying. He nodded. He was responding. He could hear them. Alethea and I told him we loved him over and over, and his head moved to one side and then the other. He could most definitely hear us. I felt as though I couldn't bear to watch the procedure. I paced the hall. I walked in and out of the room what seemed like fifty times, secretly hoping it would happen when I was in the hall, so I didn't have to see. The suspense and the anticipation made my heart pound. Alethea, in her immoveable bravery, never left his side. Ultimately, I had to watch.

I shall never forget the removal of Jacob's breathing tube as he was extubated. The look on his face reflected discomfort, exhaustion, pain, confusion, elation, relief, agony, disorientation, joy, and sadness all at the same time, if that's even possible. When the tube came out, his face contorted as if he were about to unleash the mother of all sobbing howls, but there was only silence. Moments later, however, there came a series of raspy coughs and sobs. My heart was breaking at his discomfort, and yet at the same time, I was elated beyond description that my son was breathing. He was living. Jake was breathing!

A supplemental oxygen mask was immediately placed over Jacob's face as, even in the best-case scenario, it would be some time before he'd be able to breathe room air. This was difficult. It added to the fact that not only was he physically unable to speak after having the breathing tube jammed between his vocal cords for weeks, but he also still had a tremendous amount of medicine streaming through his body retarding all his faculties.

He desperately tried to communicate, but we couldn't understand what he was saying, especially from behind the mask. I tried to read his lips, but his long-awaited and precious breaths fogged up the mask. The only phrase we could make out, and it was an entirely welcome one, was "I love you." The words came out like grunts and moans, and his speech was as if he had a mouthful of gauze. We could happily decipher those words though. He said it over and over again. We did too. Tears flowed.

Although he continued to try to communicate, it was virtually impossible to interpret what he was trying to say. My penchant for getting angry when someone I love is hurting reared its head immediately. I was so frustrated trying to understand what he was saying. I kept asking the nurses if he was in pain. I wanted them to do something. Fortunately, in short order, one of the seasoned nurses was able to satisfy me that, with the amount of drugs which were in his body, pain wasn't an issue. In her experience, she was able to decipher what he was trying to communicate. He had to go to the bathroom. He was riled up that there were people around, and he didn't know what to do. It had to be explained to him, to whatever extent he could understand, that he was catheterized and he had a diaper on, and to just let it go.

It wasn't lost on me that after three weeks of being unconscious, under heavy sedation, and suffering long-term, significant systemic oxygen deprivation, and after experiencing several episodes that required heroic efforts to save his life, and with us wondering what his mental capabilities might be when he woke that, of all things, he was worried about pooping in front of other people. This, I thought, was a tremendously positive sign. We laughed, and we cried. I am quite unable to describe the gamut of emotions that washed over me.

I called several family members and close friends in rapid succession. I shouted into my phone, "Jake is breathing! I'll call you back!" and then I called the next person. I called the Souza-Baranowski Correctional Center where my brother, Brian, served as a Sergeant. I had spoken to him earlier, and he made me promise to call him when Jake was extubated to give him an update. I was patched through to the telephone in his assigned area where he took the call. I told him Jacob was breathing on his own. He shouted it out to his co-workers, many of whom I knew, and all of whom had been closely following Jacob's saga. Cheers went up.

I shared the best Facebook post I could possibly imagine:

Jacob is breathing! Jacob is breathing! Thank God the Father Almighty! He is breathing!

Jacob's Army excitedly responded by lighting up the internet with joy and by spreading the word of his healing. We would quickly realize, however, that Jacob wasn't waking up from an afternoon nap. I don't know what I thought, but I tried to speak to him as if he were going to respond and tell me about his day. I asked him questions. I told him things. The fact that he was able to tell us he loved us apparently gave me a false sense of expedience. He came in and out of a sleeplike state. His eyes frequently rolled back. Moments punctuated by sounds, words, and movement were followed by periods of silence and stillness.

We were at once both thrilled and terrified. Though I knew the nature of the situation and though I was aware that progress would be painstakingly slow, I couldn't resist the desire to want things to move more quickly. I reluctantly accepted the disappointment and the reality that they wouldn't. Still, he was alive, saved by a miracle. He was breathing. For that we were indescribably grateful. We were humbled in the truest sense of the word by answered prayer. We stood in awe of the miracle we were witnessing. Alethea and I shared many tearful looks and nods which, as they had so many times during this journey, didn't require words. Our son would live!

The medical team was as excited as we were, though they repeatedly warned that the marathon continued and we were far from sprinting toward the front door of the hospital. We would need to tip-toe through minefields that the coming days would bring and which, they said, they expected to be fraught with challenges and pitfalls.

We were told that it would likely take weeks for Jacob to recover enough to be moved off the ICU, and they reminded us that placing him back on a ventilator might be necessary, dependent upon how his lungs responded. The ensuing days would prove to be slow moving and, at times, agonizing.

The level of Jacob's lucidity improved ever so slowly. He still required a battery of medications and significant support. Many sets of eyes constantly monitored him. People were ready to pounce at the sign of any deterioration in his status. Alethea and I anxiously and desperately attempted to understand any sort of communication he offered. We jumped at anything that made us believe he was in discomfort or pain. He was frail and weak, and it seemed like it took an exhausting effort for him just to roll his head to one side or to slightly lift an arm.

Jacob's physical appearance was alarming. His mop of a hairdo hung over his face and spread across his pillow. In recent months he'd preferred to grow his hair long. During his hospitalization, Alethea would frequently wash his hair and comb it neatly, and we considered many times cutting it when he was in his coma and then telling him, once he finally awoke, with our fingers crossed behind our backs, that it had been medically necessary to do so. Anticipating the adolescent wrath that might follow, however, we decided against it. Despite my military-style preference, I found him to be handsome with the long hair anyway.

His formerly full face was now sunken and pale. His athletic and muscular body had been reduced to skin and bones. I had to hold back tears whenever there was a need to expose his legs. His once powerful legs gave the appearance that someone had wrapped delicate fabric around a pair of baseball bats. He was skeletal. Holding his hand and feeling his fingers in mine felt as if I were holding a bundle of brittle twigs encased in rice paper. His feet and knees appeared abnormally large contrasted against the slivers that were now his shins. His wrist bones protruded almost as if they were deformed. When he held up an arm, his hand dangled as if it were barely attached.

The sinister illness that attacked Jacob had whittled him to the bone. He was a strong and vibrant teenage boy, weighing one hundred forty-six pounds before being hospitalized. His weight was now measured under ninety-six pounds. In less than a month, his sickness stole fully one-third of his body weight. I struggled to imagine the battles and processes within his body that must have occurred to enable that to be possible. The beaming joy that we shared in celebrating the fact that our son was breathing didn't alleviate his overall medical condition. The medical team walked a tightrope to keep him stable and ensure that his lungs were continuing to work.

The following evening, the hesitant caution of the medical staff proved to be wise. Jacob developed a massive, life-threatening pneumothorax. Air once again gathered into his chest cavity. Doctors and nurses quickly sprang into action. I was reminded of the scene in the movie *The Perfect Storm* where the crew of the Andrea Gale found themselves amid towering seas in a treacherous storm in the North Atlantic. For a brief moment the clouds parted to reveal the sunshine above, as if somewhere just beyond their grasp, peace and tranquility awaited them. The sun shone brightly in a fleeting moment of calmness, only to have the bruised and villainous clouds close up again and engulf them in terror. The storm was swallowing us up yet again.

Doctors had to perform another surgical procedure and insert another chest tube into Jacob's side to relieve the deadly condition. This time, though, he wasn't comatose, so he had an awareness of what was going on around him. Thankfully he was quickly stabilized. Through the weaning of his medications, he was becoming ever so gradually more coherent. His words were few and they weren't easily understood. After he recovered from the pneumothorax and was stable again, however, he looked at me pointedly and clearly asked, "What's next?" as if he were saying, "Let's go. Bring it on."

Medical staff told us he would be a long way from speaking,

yet he had numerous moments of lucidity and communication that lit up our faces. The pneumothorax aside, they continued to comment on the unlikely and remarkable nature of his healing and the progress he was making.

He slowly began to grasp his surroundings. He saw the garland we decorated his bed with and realized it was Christmas time. We were cautious, though, about the rate at which we should divulge his situation to him. We didn't know how appropriate it was to tell him about all that happened and how grave his situation had been and still was, for fear of frightening him. He was so emotional. We weren't sure what he could handle.

I tried to see if he had any concept of the time that had passed, but I couldn't really tell. He loosely clutched a football signed by his teammates. More accurately, it rested in the crook of his arm. He would break long periods of silence with welcome but brief questions and phrases. He was returning to us slowly but surely. When we told him about all the people praying for him, he cried and cried. He intuitively knew he was in rough shape. We had no idea what he remembered, though, and we weren't at all sure of his overall cognitive ability. Each time we asked him a question and he had some level of response, we struggled to assess whether his sometimes strange, drawn out, and garbled responses were induced by medication, or if he had lost any of his mental or speech faculties.

The following day Jacob was breathing well enough and his oxygen levels held strong enough for the doctors to remove his supplemental oxygen mask. Nick, Bella, and Sammy came to visit. They hadn't been to Boston at all. Alethea and I couldn't bear to have them see their brother the way he was. But now he was awake.

Any parent of multiple children is familiar with the daily domestic sibling battles. Someone was always not getting along to some degree with someone else. When those kids walked into the room, though, it was the most tender moment I'd ever witnessed between my children. When Jacob saw them, he reached out his frail arms and could do nothing but cry. They all leaned in for hugs. It made my heart melt. By the end of the day, he was able to lucidly communicate that he wanted to go home. Tears fell all around.

On New Year's Eve day, Jacob's strides were phenomenal. He began to speak to us, and we enjoyed true communication for the first time. I tried to explain the chain of events, but I struggled with where to begin and how to properly and effectively explain it to him. I brought my notebook to him and showed him the calendar I'd created, showing the dates spanning both his time in Worcester and in Boston. It showed where he had been, which unit and which room he was in, and what his status was. I told him he'd been asleep for three weeks. In disbelief, he simply said, "No. I wasn't."

I softly, almost apologetically, showed him my notes and weighed it against the calendar on the wall. I showed him that he'd been brought to the hospital in Worcester on the fifth day of December. I showed him that it was now the last day of December, and Christmas had passed several days prior. He had a difficult time processing it, and I did my best to use dialogue that I hoped wouldn't upset him. I told him of the love, the people, the prayer, and the miracle. I wish I recalled his words. All I can recall are the hugs and the tears.

His speech remained slurred and slow, and it took effort for him to form the words he wished to speak. I had to fight not to finish his words for him, which I could tell was frustrating him. He would shake his head at me when I presumed wrongly what he wanted to say. He had very limited gross motor skills and zero fine motor skills.

He could balance the football in his arm. He could reach out for a hug and even offer up his hand for a fist bump, although he

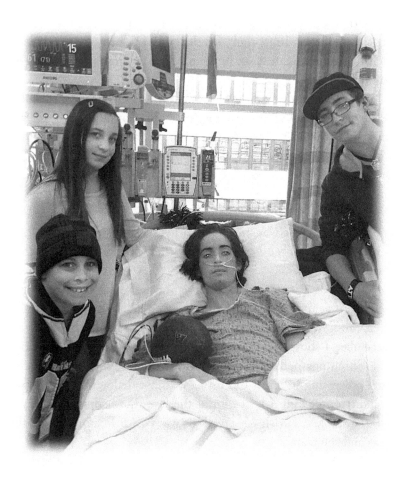

couldn't close his fist all the way. He couldn't sit or stand. He couldn't use his hands or fingers. Speaking exhausted him. I shuddered at the obvious scope of the recovery ahead.

Physical therapists came in to evaluate his motor skills and told us they would come back twice daily. As testament to his fighting spirit, when he heard the therapist talking to me and Alethea, Jake said, "Three." I asked him what he'd said. Slowly and deliberately he said, "Come back three times a day, please." Here was a kid who couldn't even hold a pencil asking for the therapists to come back three times a day instead of twice. Soon, they brought him a special iPad that was designed to be used with very little manual dexterity. He struggled to perform the functions, but he did it. In fact, the machine wasn't working properly, and he got frustrated. I knew my boy was back. I smiled from ear to ear.

More family and friends visited on New Year's Day. By the end of the day, Jacob managed to be able to use his thumb to give a thumbs up sign. We'd decorated his room with a paper chain of messages created by his classmates. Each loop of paper on the chain contained a message from someone. As he became more aware of his surroundings, he noticed it strung along the ceiling and around the doors and windows and asked us to read him the messages. We read several of them, but he insisted we read each one and tell him who it was from. I do believe we read every single one. There were hundreds. It seemed to energize him.

In no time at all, when the therapists came in, he asked if he could try to stand. We were told that such a thing was a long way off. But true to his stubbornness, he stood (aided) for fifteen seconds. On their way out of the room, as simple as it may seem for someone to be able to stand with two other people holding them up, they told us that they wouldn't have expected him to be able to do that for some time to come.

"He's a fighter," they said. "He's a strong one."

My brother Eric, the de facto spokesman of Jacob's Army

asked him if he wanted to say hello to the masses of his followers so they could see how well he was doing, and he obliged. So Eric filmed a short video. As excited as we were at the time, the video is heart-wrenching to watch. Had I not been so enveloped in the excitement we were experiencing, I wouldn't have allowed it, realizing now how premature it was and how graphically it depicted his frail condition. Fighting to speak coherently, Jacob thanked everyone for their prayers and said he would be home soon. I can hardly watch it to this day.

The next few days marked a period of joy and anxious fear. They were full of challenges, conquests, and cheers. Visitors came to see and pray. Doctors continued to stand and nod in their amazement. Alethea and I told Jake his story. We told him everything from the beginning. He was overcome. He recalled nothing from the time he was wheeled into the hospital in Worcester until our conversation on New Year's Eve day. He didn't recall the days in Worcester before he was sedated. He didn't recall waking up when he was extubated, nor any of our first conversations. All told, he'd lost twenty-six days of his life, which he would never regain.

He progressed at a stunning rate though. He soon began to stand unaided for several seconds at a time. Each time it taxed him to exhaustion, and he promptly slept for considerable periods. The healing was occurring before our eyes. He began to eat small amounts of soft food and recovered enough dexterity to be able to feed himself a spoonful of pudding.

Each visit with friends or family fired up his passion. His school chums showed up and cheered him on. Randy, the unofficial president of the WPHL, and the one who dubbed him the Hurricane, arrived at the hospital wearing full hockey gear. He delivered Jacob his own, brand new hockey stick, making him promise that he'd be on the ice by next winter. Appropriately, it was a Warrior hockey stick. Jacob was thrilled. He clutched the stick in his bed for days.

On the fifth day of January, although he was still in serious medical condition and had many hills to climb, and although he still had chest tubes protruding from his body to manage potentially critical pneumothorax conditions, his incredible progress warranted his transfer out of the intensive care unit. What the medical team had cautioned us would take weeks and weeks, happened in only nine days. He was discharged from the ICU and transferred to the hospital's 7 West wing. I gleefully posted a photograph of his empty ICU room with all its machines and monitors rendered blank and silent. They were required no longer. It was a good day. It was a very good day.

Tough days would follow, though. It became immediately apparent that the steepest challenge of the next leg of our journey would be something we really hadn't forecast as a hurdle and something which had been entirely absent to that point. Previously Jake was suspended in a coma and unconscious. Now, however, he was awake.

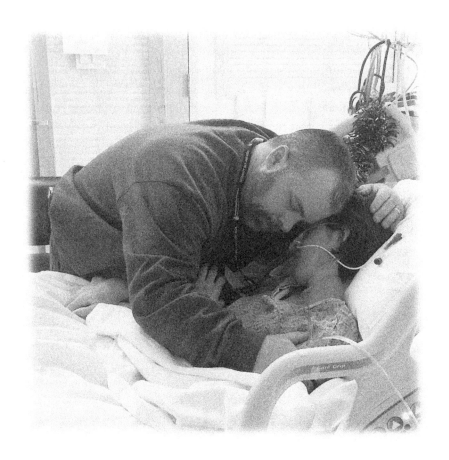

SEVENTEEN

BERNIE THE SLOTH AND GARDEN HOSES

Whereas previously Jacob was somewhere beyond the conscious world and couldn't communicate, he was now actively in the battle with us. Before he woke up, the pain was mine and Alethea's alone. Now it was all of ours to bear together. For all the tumult and heartache involved in the previous three weeks, at least during that time we didn't have to see our son in pain. Watching him struggle and battle through the days and weeks ahead would prove to test the limits of our endurance as parents.

Chest tubes are a painful undertaking. They're painful to have inserted, frequently painful for the time that they're in use, and painful to have removed. A chest tube is a rigid tube inserted through the skin between two ribs and into the patient's chest cavity. Even slight movements can cause sharp and intense pain.

Although he was breathing, Jake was only able to do so because of the function the chest tubes were serving. The tubes allowed the air that leaked from his lungs to escape his body and prevented it from gathering in his chest cavity, where it would again collapse the lungs. Without them, his lungs couldn't properly expand.

His left lung, for reasons unknown, suffered more damage than the right one, which continued to hold. His lungs couldn't expand nearly as much as healthy lungs do, but they could expand enough for him to breathe. Although he was miraculously healing against all medical odds, his lungs were still significantly damaged and had a long way to go before they could function without the need for medical intervention. He would need to embark on his recovery with what amounted to garden hoses protruding out of his body, limiting his movement and causing him constant discomfort and pain.

Jacob's recovery was brutal. It was no less taxing than when he'd been knocking on death's door, although in different ways. The roller coaster ride continued. There were good days and great days. There were also, regrettably, many decidedly awful days. He had a speech therapist, physical therapists, and occupational therapists. He had a nutritionist, a pulmonary team, and a radiology team who had to position him for x-rays, sometimes several times a day. The days were exhausting. Mental health counselors visited nearly daily. Underneath the smiles and the joy of Jacob's survival lurked the sometimes harsh and ugly consequences resulting from enduring significant trauma. All this was topped off by the fact that, for all intents and purposes, his body was addicted to the heavy drugs that had been streaming through his system for weeks. As a result, he suffered the unholy and miserable symptoms of being weaned from narcotics.

We worked on his dexterity daily. Getting to the point where he could use his fingers to text his friends was a major accomplishment. One day I had a small foam football that fit in the palm of my hand, probably the size of a mouse and not weighing more than a couple of ounces. I tossed it to him from the foot of his bed. When he tried to toss it back, it dribbled out of his hand and onto his lap and rolled to his feet. Moments like that clearly illustrated how far there was to go. Sometimes he was able to laugh at his situation. Other times he cried or was scared or downright angry. He often reached out to me and asked me to pray with him.

His speech improved little by little. Although we could communicate, he was often frustrated by the fact that I had to ask him to repeat nearly everything he said because I could hardly understand what he said. Sitting up in bed or in a chair was difficult, even for a few seconds. It wasn't made any easier by the various tubes and wires that were still connected to him. Standing for any amount of time utterly exhausted him. The medical tethers would get hooked on his bed and tug at him, sometimes causing him pain. To make things worse, just about every day at some point I would inadvertently step on his tubing and wiring or kick his suction machine over.

Even after he began to eat food, he continued to require a nasogastric (NG) tube to provide him with constant nutrition as his body had suffered so egregiously. At night his NG tube would leak while he slept, and he'd wake up soaked in a nasty brown mess. He cursed that tube to hell, calling it his dog leash. Toileting was difficult. He couldn't ambulate to the bathroom. That meant a portable toilet, which is simply unpleasant for everyone involved.

His body was still sick and frail. It became a daily challenge to deal with the frustration of a once strong young man who used to hurl fastballs at upwards of eighty miles per hour, but who now couldn't even stand on his own, and who needed significant help simply to use the toilet.

Sometimes, apparently for no particular reason at all, Jacob would become overcome by maddening itching all over his body. We never found out if it was related to medication, linens, food, or some other source. When it struck, it struck hard. He was inconsolable. We bought all new linens and stopped using the hospital sheets in case it was due to whatever cleaning agents they used. We never really figured that one out. It was just one of the "bonuses" as we called them. It felt like the tests just kept coming.

We quizzed the doctors as to how much longer they thought he would need each piece of equipment, each medication, each tube and wire and machine. There were never definitive answers because so much was unknown. They were very cautious with Jacob because they still really had no idea what happened to him or what was going to transpire moving forward. Jake and I would bet on things like when his next chest tube could be removed or when he would no longer need the NG tube. We looked ahead and itemized the things we'd do when he got home.

We tried to keep our eyes forward and dealt with every blow one by one. It wasn't unusual to have a terrific day, followed by a terrible night, or vice versa. One look from my wife or me when we relieved each other for hospital duty was all that was needed to see what kind of day or night he'd had. After a long shift with Jacob at the hospital, there were multiple times when Alethea would arrive, and my exit would be swift. It was all so very stressful now that he was awake, in discomfort, in pain, and experiencing all the emotions associated with the trial he'd endured and was still enduring. His consciousness was challenging to say the very least.

After about a week into his recovery, as we settled into our daily routine, dealt with the regular issues and minor disasters, and began to realistically look ahead to one day bringing him home, Jake's lungs loudly announced that they weren't quite finished testing us just yet. His breathing suddenly and rapidly deteriorated, and he was rushed to surgery, where yet another emergency procedure was performed and the insertion of still another chest tube was required, and he was back in the ICU. Thankfully, he was quickly stabilized and returned to the floor on 7 West, along with another new garden hose. Periodic, life-threatening conditions became just another hurdle and part of the routine.

He soon graduated to eating small amounts of some more solid food but hadn't yet been able to reclaim the ability to swallow sufficiently enough to eat real food. It was a glorious day when he finally passed the swallow tests. He was so thin. I couldn't wait for him to eat and to start packing on the pounds he'd lost. His physical appearance was particularly troubling for me.

There was a Bertucci's restaurant across the street from the hospital. Once I received the approval, I ran down and bought him a giant plate of ravioli. He inhaled it. It became a nearly nightly ritual. Jacob ate so much ravioli in the coming weeks, it's a wonder he can even stand the sight of it now.

We worked hard every day. Jake was determined to get better. He battled through his handicaps. We did everything we could think of to exercise his limbs and to strengthen him. He could sit and stand for increasingly longer periods. Like when he was a baby, we cheered at his first steps. I admired his courage and tried to sympathize with his frustrations. I pushed him because I felt it was my job, but there were many times I needed to back off, and I failed to recognize it. He let me know it.

Passing time, once again, became a daily task. We played video games, watched the Boston Bruins and the NFL playoffs, read books and magazines, and listened to music. I told him every joke I knew. I taught him how to play cribbage. It took a long time for him to gain enough dexterity to effectively shuffle a deck of cards. After he did, he practiced dozens of card tricks. We told stories and talked about life and death and baseball and girls. We learned a lot about one another, having so much time together in close quarters. We made the best of everything when spirits were high. When they were low, we hunkered down, tried to focus, and prayed. I fed him every piece of fatherly advice I could possibly muster. Any conversation could span from being universally serious to downright superficial and sometimes inappropriate.

We played games, like thinking of how many colorful ways there are to describe the act of relieving one's self. There are many. We made fun of each other and of everyone else. We made up nicknames for every nurse and housekeeper. Some were less than flattering, but they certainly weren't meant to be hurtful. There was a doctor who saw Jake frequently who spoke in a thick Russian accent. She was less than gentle with her pulling and prodding and manipulations. Whenever I saw her coming, I would channel my best Russian voice and tell Jacob, "I must break you." He knew who was coming when I said that, and he laughed heartily every time.

There was a regular nurse with an uncommonly loud voice. We called her Nurse Bose because it sounded like she must have had speakers hidden somewhere. I tried to make Jake laugh as often as I could. We pulled up Three Stooges and Abbott & Costello acts from online. I introduced him to the classic Who's on First? skit.

The nurses were awesome. They were good sports and indulged our tomfoolery. One of them was less than pleased one day when she asked me to help her unplug an electric cord attached to Jake's bed. When I did, I pretended rather loudly and dramatically (and quite convincingly I must say) that I got electrocuted. She nearly had a heart attack. We had fake poop, provided by one of Jacob's arguably twisted relatives, which looked very realistic. We'd leave it in strategic locations designed for unwitting people to find. We invented funny songs. We had a lot of fun.

We temporarily adopted a stuffed sloth named Bernie from Jacob's Aunt Rebecca. We positioned Bernie daily in different places and with all manner of hospital accessories. He became our mascot. Bernie found his way all over the hospital for cameo appearances. Jake would get mad at me when I made him laugh so hard that his tubes moved and hurt him. My father and my brothers were little help in that regard. Whenever they came to visit, it was basically like a custom-tailored comedy act. It was worse if they came as a group. When they did, we could hear them coming from all the way down the hall. We laughed a lot. Laughter was an integral part of recovery. We thoroughly enjoyed every minute of laughter because we'd learned that frustration and pain were waiting around every corner, lurking like a predator in the shadows. The highs and lows were extreme.

By the end of January, the right lung healed enough to have the chest tube on that side of his chest removed again. By then, he could walk a good distance down the hallway with portable suction machines attached. We even took him outside to a courtyard in a wheelchair for a brief while for his first fresh air in two months. Days moved slowly and were always predicated on routine. If ever there was a new nurse who didn't necessarily know the routine, we surely did. Jacob had no issue telling a new nurse that she was doing something wrong. The routine was then often punctuated by varying levels of emergencies, which would be brought under control, and the routine was promptly resumed.

Alethea and I traded shifts day in and day out. We missed one another very much. Jacob needed one of us to be there at all times for when bad things occurred and for when he had particularly tough days or nights. We never wanted to leave him anyway. One of us was always there, and the other was home. Sometimes we'd arrange for a meal together or even part of an evening for a few hours while one of our family members was with Jake.

It wasn't long before we determined the best times of day for one of us to come or go so we would face the least traffic. When I was headed into the city, I'd call Alethea when I got to Storrow Drive and was approaching the Fenway area so I could tell her it was alright for her to leave because I'd be there shortly. Sometimes we'd pass one another as she left and I approached. We'd make eye contact, and it seemed as if we exchanged an hour of hugs and conversation in those fleeting seconds. We were exhausted in every conceivable way. It was the kind of tired that doesn't go away with physical rest.

The time in the hospital wasn't the only time that needed to be contended with. There was also the time at home. We essentially had gone from a two-parent home to a one-parent home since we were never home together. Alethea and I were rarely in the same location. After dealing with issues at home and taking care of the other kids, there was still my insomnia and the night time that needed to be dealt with.

Nights at home were long for me. I didn't sleep much as I always had one ear waiting for the phone to ring if something bad happened, and I always had a quick escape planned if I needed to rush to Boston.

One afternoon when I was at home, I was standing by the kitchen window and noticed it was really ugly. The caulking was weathered and worn. The wood was old, scratched, and peeling. There were cracks in the seams, and I could feel the breeze coming through from outside. I grabbed a small flat bar from my tool bucket and pried off a piece of trim. There was no insulation behind the trim in the gap between the window and the rough opening. In minutes I stripped the window. It ended up being one of those "What did I just do?" moments.

I went to the store and bought some materials to re-trim the window. I called my dear friend Mark, whom I affectionately call Meatball, and I borrowed his nail gun. I watched some You Tube videos, educated myself a little bit, and away I went. In no time at all, I had a newly trimmed and insulated window. The next day, once I'd caulked and painted the new trim with brilliant, glossy white paint, it stood out. It looked fantastic. But that just made everything else look old and gross. And so it began.

Over the rest of Jacob's hospitalization, I slowly and methodically removed, repaired, and replaced every single piece of trim on the first floor of my home. Each piece I replaced and painted made the piece next to it look terrible. I had to continue, at the risk of my OCD tendencies causing me serious grief. I would ultimately replace every piece of door trim, window trim, and baseboard. I rebuilt the archway going into the living room and a bay window in the family room. I even trimmed out the fireplace. These days, every time I need to borrow a tool from Meatball, he asks with a grin if he'll be able to get it back in less than three months.

The new trim also made the old, battered, and worn baseboard heater covers look particularly nasty. So those had to go as well, as did the old, roughed up doors to the bathroom, the basement, the pantry, and the trash closet. I wasn't very good at it, as I'd never done it before. As I went along, though, my skills improved. It was a productive way to pass time. I began to look forward to putting the kids to bed during the nights I was home so I could continue my projects.

I started looking for things to fix, something I hadn't done a great deal of in the past. Then I decided Jake needed a new room when he got home, so I remodeled his room. I painted and repaired things. I redecorated from top to bottom with new bed linen, Bruins curtains, Casting Crowns poster, Red Sox and Patriots signs, and an American flag with a soldier on it.

Our drum kit was in the middle of his room. Earlier that year, before Jacob's hospitalization, I'd experienced a little bit of a mid-life crisis. I'd been a drummer when I was a youngster but hadn't played since I was in the military. I got the itch again, found a great deal on a sweet kit on Craig's List, and perhaps without my wife's complete approval, I came home with a new set of drums. Jacob thought it was cool that his Dad could play the drums. It's like riding a bike. I picked it back up in no time. The only place the drum kit would fit, though, was in Jacob's bedroom. He watched me and learned to play, and he loved it.

So I took the opportunity to spruce up our drum kit. There was a music store a few blocks from the hospital. On several occasions when I could eventually leave Jake while he was sleeping or watching television, I walked there to get some air and returned to the hospital room with a new cymbal or a stand or some other accessory for our kit, much to his delight. Anything I could find to do to pass the time was the name of the game. I polished the cymbals to a high shine and made sure he had a cool bedroom when he came home.

Despite the many smiles, positive days, and great strides, the progress was slow and agonizing. Jacob's Army never left our side, though. They were ever present with encouragement, prayer, and all manner of assistance, both at home and at the hospital. People continued to simply be awesome, and it caused me to see everyone I met in a new light.

Where previously I routinely and purposely avoided conversation with strangers, I now welcomed it. I met wonderful souls in the hospital. There's a kindred spirit between parents of sick children, and it doesn't take much for them to be able to connect. I met people from all over the country, and the world for that matter, whose children's ailments brought them to Boston Children's Hospital.

We shared our trials, our frustrations, and our grief. It served not only as fellowship but oftentimes also as a reality check. I didn't have to look far or long to find someone whose situation made ours pale in comparison. There were admittedly times when I felt a little sorry for myself due to what we were going through. Usually, though, I quickly found someone whose story made Jacob's ordeal seem like dealing with a hangnail.

One day in the laundry room, I met a woman who was clearly tired and weary. We commiserated during our conversation, and I complained a bit about being far from home for so many weeks and months and living out of a clothes hamper and a wall locker in a hospital room. She told me she knew what I meant. She'd been there for four months. She was from North Carolina, a thousand miles from her home, and there I was complaining about being ninety minutes from my home. At least I could drive home. I felt like a dope.

On another occasion I struck up a conversation with a woman from the Midwest. She inquired about my son, and when I indulged her and told her about our journey, she listened intently to every detail with genuine interest and empathy. She placed her hand on my shoulder and offered her reassurance and support.

When I, in turn, asked about her ordeal, she explained to me that she and her husband had been there for thirteen months and that their daughter had undergone eleven heart and brain surgeries. When I asked how old her daughter was, she told me she was thirteen months old. My heart sank. I vowed I would never complain about anything again. I like to think I've largely kept that promise. When I do catch myself complaining about something, I'm usually quick to correct it.

I now look at simple conversations with people much differently than I ever did before. People that I historically overlooked with disinterest while I selfishly focused on my own life, my own little world, and my own issues and needs, had suddenly become real. They became stories I wanted to hear. Shamefully, I realized that in the past I had judged people, sometimes on their appearance alone. I learned to embrace the idea that everyone has a struggle, and everyone has a story. I eagerly engaged people whom I'd previously deliberately avoided.

Frequently while at the hospital, when there was an opportunity, I'd go for a walk to stretch my legs and my mind when Jake looked like he seemed to be doing well. I stopped at a corner barbershop one morning to get myself cleaned up a bit. The barber was a foreigner with heavily accented but understandable English. I probably spent five minutes just trying to properly pronounce his name, which regrettably has long since escaped my memory. We talked through a long and relaxing haircut. We talked about each other's names and our ethnic heritage. We talked about food and about Boston. I must have needed to vent because I told him all about my son, something I would have never done in the past. Sometime during the conversation, I laughed about what a train wreck and a ragamuffin Jacob looked like after so many weeks in the hospital, without a real bath or grooming. I commented how I wished I could wheel him right out the front door of the hospital and down there for a haircut.

One evening there was a knock on the door of Jake's hospital room. I opened it expecting one of our regular visitors or medical staff. But it was my new barber friend, portable haircut kit in hand, standing there with Jake's nurse. After working all day, he closed his shop and came up to find us in the hospital. The nurse asked if it was alright if he came in.

I couldn't believe he actually came. The nurse carefully set Jacob up in a chair with a portable suction machine for his chest tubes. This man took a solid hour out of his time with his own family to carefully cut my son's hair as if he were an artist making a sculpture.

He talked and joked with Jacob and shared many stories. When he was done, he adamantly refused any payment whatsoever, packed his things, and left with a smile. I learned to love people in an entirely different way than I ever had before. Though I would never reasonably expect to cross his path again, the barber, as so many other people had, touched my life if only for a brief moment.

People kept us going. Our army remained in formation through the long weeks of recovery. They were as resilient as Jacob's lungs were stubborn. Family and friends visited often. Group visits from Jake's pals were some of the best therapy there was. The support never waned. I looked forward to whoever our next guest would be and to the conversation and fellowship they would bring with them. I continued to bring cards to Jacob that had been mailed to our home daily, and we read them together. We found many ways to enjoy ourselves between the various and continuing unpleasant experiences.

In early February, we had the luxury of being able to have a Super Bowl party in Jake's room. Our beloved New England Patriots had made it to the big game once again, and what a treat that was given the circumstances. Jacob was at a stage of recovery where he could thoroughly enjoy the game. I brought Nicholas and their close friend Kyle to Boston. We ordered out for pizza and chicken wings, and we whooped it up. We drank root beer like pirates drink rum. It was the most exciting Super Bowl ever with the greatest ending in Super Bowl history.

We cheered and hollered and threw footballs around. We knocked things over and garnered the attention of more than one nurse and doctor. I ran down the hall and slid on my knees when the Patriots scored, much to the delight of other patients, who thought I was a bit crazy. I lost my mind when Gronk hauled in a touchdown pass, and I spiked the football so hard that I actually hurt myself. The ball ricocheted around like something out of a Bugs Bunny cartoon and I knocked over an IV pole. They don't fall quietly. It was a fine night.

We made it our goal to have fun whenever we could. There was a woman who came around and brought musical instruments for the patients to play. Jacob tried several of them. As he became more mobile, we'd roam the halls with our garden hoses in tow and our suction machines whirring away. There was a game room we'd visit where we could play air hockey. I saw every little thing as physical therapy, so I pushed him to do as much as he could do. With Jake taking part in normal activities, we lulled ourselves into a false sense of security that the worst was over.

By mid-February, though, several attempts to seal Jake's lungs had failed, and air escaping into his chest cavity proved to be an insurmountable problem. Though the doctors had put it off for as long as they could, to allow for as much healing as they could, they couldn't delay any longer and announced that they had to perform lung surgery, and they even spoke of transplants. The chief of pulmonary surgery, like several other doctors before him, commented on the uniqueness of Jacob's condition, saying that he'd never seen anything quite like the damage he had suffered or his incredible recovery.

Although the surgery was initially declared a total success, the fight would continue. After a grueling recovery from the surgery, which we hoped was paving the road home, the left lung failed again, creating yet another life-threatening situation that resulted in emergency surgeries on back-to-back days. As a bonus, each one was dramatically punctuated by a massive allergic reaction, causing Jacob so much pain and agony that I couldn't take it and had to excuse myself several times to punch the walls in a nearby bathroom. It was awful. The enemy would simply not let us go.

More arduous recovery and therapy followed. The medical team members resigned themselves to the fact that an even slower healing process was the only option. So, Jake soldiered on with multiple chest tubes inserted, healing a little more every day. Each day was a hurdle. I filled him with ravioli and steak and other goodies from Bertucci's. Every day I went for walks to deal with my own anxieties. Jacob was usually the beneficiary, as I would always return with treats for him. Shamrock shakes from McDonald's were a favorite, and they were packed with calories. My mission to fatten him up continued.

We walked farther every day. We began to climb stairs and go outside when we could. His dexterity and coordination returned. His speech was now normal. His systems were good. He was making real progress. Jake's teachers at school coordinated with Nick (who was a grade behind him). Nick would bring Jake's schoolwork home with him, and we, in turn, would bring it to Jake in Boston so he could try to keep pace with his classmates and make up for the lost time. The hospital provided a tutor who worked with Jacob several times a week. Jake was getting ready to finish Middle School, so he applied to a coveted local vocational high school and went through the interview process from his hospital bed.

By mid-March the frustration mounted as he was progressing wonderfully in all other areas, but he was still being held back by the tubes and wires that bound him and the mechanisms that kept his lungs expanded. Wary of more failures, the doctors needed to be doubly sure before attempting to remove any of them again, lest another surgery would result and, perhaps even worse, one of his nasty reactions to anesthesia. Whenever the pulmonary team came into the room, we waited with baited breath to hear whether or not it was time. We became experts in their language, and we were keenly attuned to the words to listen for. Before they were even finished talking, we already knew what the decisions were for the day.

Sometimes Jacob's frustration and anxiety would erupt when they informed us they would have to wait and check again in a couple days or a week. There came a point when, without Jacob's knowledge, we directed the doctors not to discuss his situation inside the room because he grew so upset, thinking he was never leaving the hospital. We made a sign for the outside of the door directing that all medical conversation take place outside of the room. I was usually able to hide the sign from his view if we were passing by, but one day he saw it. He let Mom and I have it pretty good for that.

As they had been on so many occasions over the course of the weeks and months, our emotions were mixed and at odds. Every day we were hopeful that the time had come to try to remove his chest tubes once and for all, and we were eternally grateful for the healing, but at the same time, we were scared that it would be time. We were scared of the unknown. On the fifteenth of March, it was time.

That day, as the pulmonary team evaluated the situation, they called for other doctors to consult with. Still more came. They came in and out of the room. They checked and re-checked everything. After much discussion among themselves and then with Mom and Dad, and with Jacob as well (because there was no longer a sign), it was declared time to test the lung again. The months-long saga had come down to this defining moment.

Doctors first removed the smaller chest tube. I will never get used to seeing my child in pain. I do believe that I never wish to see a chest tube inserted or removed from one of my children ever again. The procedure was successful and had the desired effect as it pertained to lung expansion and no new pneumothoraxes forming. It was a great sign. But the bigger garden hose remained. The following several days were heavy with anticipation. While we waited for them to tell us they were ready to remove the final tube, we half expected the lung to collapse again and require re-insertion of another tube. This time, though, the lung didn't fail. The bad news didn't come.

Four days later, the pulmonary team and the doctors on Jacob's floor huddled again and declared the lung was ready for the final test. They would remove the final chest tube the following day. The only tether tying Jake to that hospital would be cut. That night was excruciatingly long. Jacob asked me to pray with him and told me he simply couldn't endure another setback. His tank was empty. He'd fought battle after battle. He had taken all the coaching, the counseling, the mothering, the fathering, the hoping, and the praying that he could take. There was no way he could deal with even one more episode of me telling him he had one more obstacle in front him and that he needed to keep on fighting. He had taken a beating. He had suffered. It needed to be over. He needed to be set free once and for all.

Preparations were made the next morning. Around midday the final garden hose was carefully, but painfully, removed from Jacob's body. We waited in stone cold silence. He breathed. We breathed. No alarms sounded. No one came running. No somber and apologetic medical faces or voices presented themselves. An hour passed and then two. Mom and I paced. Jacob, so accustomed to bad news, declared he knew it didn't work. He'd become conditioned to expect the worst. He said something didn't feel right. He said he could feel his lungs collapsing again. He was convincing himself that the attempts had failed again. We talked him down and put on our best masks, fighting our own anxieties, and we told him there was nothing to worry about and that the lung was holding, even though we felt the same way he did.

We talked about the first things he'd do and what he would eat when he got home. I prayed that the Lord wouldn't make a liar out of me. I asked God to please not burden us again with having to tell our son one more time that he had to keep battling.

Four hours after the procedure, all was well. X-rays were taken. Everything was where it should be. The lung was holding. Nothing was wrong. For the first time, absolutely nothing was wrong.

The notion that everything was fine was so foreign to us that it was almost anticlimactic. We really didn't even know what to do. Alethea and I embraced and looked at one another, silently asking each other with our eyes if it was really over. With my heart brimming with thanks and tears in my eyes, I turned to Jacob and said, "Let's go home, son."

Preparations were made. Notifications were made. Schedules for follow-ups and all manner of medical appointments were organized. We were informed that he'd be discharged the next day. Discharged! Against all odds, Jacob finished the race. There were no more hills to climb. There were no more obstacles. The lad had finally found his way out of the woods. He found the lighthouse in the storm. Just like that, it was all over.

We were going home.

EIGHTEEN

FIRST PITCH

Alethea addressed all the logistics. I packed our belongings and called everyone I could. I'm confident that the sleep I gained that night could be measured in minutes and not hours. We watched Jacob like a hawk and looked for even the slightest hiccup. Every time he rustled in his bed, I leapt to my feet. I imagined every unsavory circumstance or occurrence that could possibly happen. Surely it couldn't be that it was really all over.

Morning came though. The sun came up. Nothing was wrong. Nothing bad happened. After the morning medical rounds were completed, the official discharge process began. It was almost impossible to think. I was excited and happy but in disbelief. Half of me was scared at the thought of leaving the safety of the hospital. We cleaned and packed and prepared. I deliberately moved around, slowly gathering our belongings, trying to act calmly and keep my cool. I attempted to keep my excitement in check and waited for whatever obstacle would present itself. Things began to look great. It was really happening.

Just to remind us, however, that control shall forever remain an illusion, right after they began the lengthy discharge process, the entire computer system for the hospital crashed. Everything came to a standstill. Suddenly we weren't going anywhere. The clouds closed up on us yet again. The storm simply refused to let us out. The computer issue caused massive complications. We waited all day. We waited for nearly eight mind-numbing hours.

There was so much involved in a discharge of this type that we had to wait. We had no choice. We made the best of it. We walked up and down the halls. We put our coats on and took them off a dozen times. We tossed the football and played soccer in the corridors. We played in the elevators. We had wheelchair races. No tubes or wires or cords dragged behind us. No machines hummed alongside. We were free from the restraints, but we were still in a cage. We dug through our bags for a deck of cards. We took as long as we possibly could to eat lunch. We cleaned the room ten times. We scoured every drawer and cubby and shelf for anything we might possibly leave behind.

Then, just when my self-discipline was expiring, and just before I reached the point of irretrievable meltdown after enduring the trial of my life, and just as I thought I would declare that we were leaving whether they discharged us or not, the lights all turned green. We were free.

On March 21, 2015, by the grace of God, I was able to keep the promise I made months before, and alongside my precious wife, I walked my boy out of that hospital. Alethea loaded Jake into the van as gingerly as she had when she did so fourteen years prior after she delivered him into this world. I thought it rather appropriate that we were headed home on the 21st day of the month with Number 21—the boy and the number—who unwittingly galvanized an entire community and an army through his suffering.

I drove with both hands on the wheel, my eyes constantly darting back and forth between the road and the rear-view mirror to watch Jacob. I stayed below the speed limit and far behind the vehicle in front of me. I drove like a teenager taking a driving test. I turned on my directional indicator a half mile in advance of when

I needed it. I came to complete stops. I had no intention of hitting so much as a crack in the road.

When I turned onto our road, I was talking to Jacob like it was any other day and we were headed home from a baseball game. In reality, it took everything I had to keep my bottom lip from quivering. Jacob arrived home to a giant banner spanning the entire front of the house which read, WELCOME HOME JACOB. Throughout Jacob's battle, some of the strangest things had hit me hard emotionally. This time it was the banner.

When I pulled up and saw the banner, even though I had hung it myself and it was just a stupid piece of vinyl, I looked at Jacob and fought back a deep sob of all-encompassing emotion that had built up inside of me and was fighting to come out. I simply couldn't believe it was all over.

Alethea walked Jacob to the door. I hung back under the guise that I was grabbing something from the back of the van. I leaned against the van and let out a guttural mixture of sounds that I was helpless to fight back. It was like a full body release.

Our family had gathered at the house. Some had been waiting for hours due to our lengthy discharge. There were enough hugs to go around. Bailey, our lovable mutt, expressed enough joy for all of us combined and thoroughly washed Jacob with kisses. After some time to let it all soak in, we gathered around the still-lit Christmas tree, dusty but beautiful, and bearing a mountain of gifts. We smiled for our family holiday photo nearly three months after Christmas had passed and at long last were able to wish everyone a very Merry Christmas from the Nano family.

Alethea and I were like nervous hens for quite some time. We watched Jake closely. Despite his new room and shiny, spruced up drum kit, he slept on the couch. He didn't feel comfortable sleeping two floors away from us. Nor did we. We found ourselves watching him all the time. If he went up the stairs to shower, I would watch him until he got all the way to the top. Alethea got

nervous whenever she couldn't see him or hear him. We stayed
close to him throughout the day and sometimes tried to hold his

elbow as he walked, just as we did in the hospital. Our hospital
habits were difficult to break, and he soon grew aggravated with us
hovering around him. We knew we had to stop treating him like a
china doll, but it wasn't easy. In the back of our minds were visions
of an ambulance ride right back to Boston. We still figured that
something had to go wrong. Nothing went wrong though. He

grew stronger every day. We let down our guard a little more each day. In about two weeks, I was confident enough to return to work. Normalcy had returned. It started to sink in with me that it might really all be over.

Jacob was initially reluctant to return to school. He feared something would happen to him and also expressed that he didn't want people looking at him weirdly or making him the center of attention. We let him get away with that for a little while and had him continue to do his schoolwork from home, but finally we told him it was time to go back. Jacob eventually returned to school as something of a local celebrity, and in short order, other than frequent medical appointments, the entire experience largely appeared to be in the rear-view mirror.

When the baseball season began, Coach had already registered him for us, but Jacob clearly couldn't play. He couldn't be kept away from the game he loved though. He was on the team and he practiced every day in some way, shape, or form, even if it just meant tossing a baseball up in the air and catching it. He vowed that he would play that season. Even though I openly agreed with him and encouraged him to work at it, I knew it wasn't possible and it made me sad. There are only so many years of youth sports, and as thankful as I was that he was alive, I felt awful that an entire year would be lost for him.

He became the unofficial dugout coach for both the school team and the town team. He couldn't play, but there he stood in the dugout wearing #21, watching the game, helping the coach, and keeping the book wearing his blue jeans, which were cinched over in the front with his belt pulled tightly to accommodate his lost inches and pounds. After each game he asked if we could go to the doctor to see if he were cleared to play. We had precisely zero expectation that it was possible and precisely zero intention of letting him trot out onto the field anyway.

Then came a late spring day when he had one of his regular

medical appointments. As usual, Jacob asked the doctor when he could play baseball. Much to our amazement, and much to Jacob's delight, the doctor shrugged his shoulders and said he didn't see any reason Jacob couldn't play ball. He saw the look of shock and concern on Mom's face and quickly added, "…that is, if it's alright with your folks."

There was no debate. Jacob was stoked. To tell him he couldn't play, after the doctor said he could, would have been an exercise in futility. His doctor cautioned him that he would need to play sparingly and that he'd need to listen to his body regarding how far he could push himself, but he said it would actually be good for him. He was easily winded and was obviously not nearly as strong as he had been before his illness. Alethea and I were terrified.

May 2, 2015 was our sixteenth wedding anniversary. It was a stunningly beautiful day, much like our wedding day was. The boys had a game. Jake was no longer wearing jeans. He was in full uniform. I was seated in the stands and Coach David (who was as nervous as we were) looked over at me from the dugout. He had previously told me that, no matter how much Jake prodded him, he wouldn't put him on the field of play until he felt he was ready, and until I specifically and expressly told him it was alright to do so. When he looked over at me that day, we both knew it was time. I nodded. He nodded. He told Jake to grab a helmet and told him he was the on-deck batter. Jake was going in. He never moved so fast in his life. Alethea squeezed my hand and cried.

Jake marched to the plate in the middle of a non-descript mid-season baseball game, yet again showing me that something I thought was impossible was possible. The bleachers erupted in cheers. I'm sure the opponents had no idea what was happening or what the commotion was all about. It was just some twig of a kid with baggy pants coming to the plate who'd been riding the pine for the entire game. Jake dug in for his first at-bat, and everyone in the stands held their collective breath.

He took a fastball down the middle for strike one. In the second it took for that first ball to travel past him, I ran through a hundred different thoughts. I truly feared he couldn't play and that he'd be devastated that he didn't have the abilities he once had. I wasn't even sure he'd be able to swing the bat effectively. I thought of what he'd been through, and there was just no way in my mind that he could resume his normal lifestyle, at least not this soon. I was preparing what I would say to him. I thought of the coaching I'd have to do in order to help him maintain some semblance of being positive.

On the second pitch, though, after not standing in a batter's box for the better part of a year, after enduring the fight of his life, and after literally having to learn how to walk again, he ripped an RBI double past the shortstop into left-center field, knocking in the go-ahead run. He took the corner at first base and hauled himself to second base with a pop-up slide like he'd been playing all year. People went nuts. It was just unbelievable.

During his next at bat, he stroked another double to straight away center field and the fans roared. Simply incredible. Jake was back. During the coming weeks, he would pinch-hit or play very sparingly in the field. His endurance had suffered significantly, and to his credit, he told Coach when he needed to come out and rest. But there he was, back on the baseball diamond. It made our hearts happy.

He continued to get stronger by the day, and it became clear that there was no turning back, despite my lingering doubts. Still, he wanted to get back on the mound. I was petrified of him pitching again. I had visions of him a taking a line drive to the chest. Coach was worried too. He didn't want to be the one to put him on the mound and have something bad happen to him.

By the time June arrived, though, his progress was so apparent that we agreed it was time. In the middle innings of a game in Westminster, Jacob had just finished throwing some warm up pitches behind the dugout. After the starting pitcher faltered, Coach trotted to the mound. Instead of looking out to the field to point out the next pitcher, he looked at me on the bleachers and then turned to the dugout where Jake was now seated on a ball bucket spitting sunflower seeds. Just like it was any other game, Coach hollered out "Nano! Let's go!"

Cheers went up, and so did I. I jumped from the stands like I'd been stung by a hornet. I took up a spot on the fence on the first base line. Alethea jumped down as well. His warm up tosses seemed like they took forever. The umpire met him at the mound and gave him the situation. There were no outs and a runner on first base.

Jacob wound up and fired a fastball right down the tube. In an instant all my fears materialized. On his very first pitch, the batter ripped the ball right back at Jacob. The opponent sharply hit a one-hop comebacker to the mound. It reached Jake in a fraction of a second.

While nightmare scenarios whisked through my mind in the blink of an eye, Jacob fielded it cleanly, trotted a few steps toward first base, and calmly slow-tossed the baseball to the first baseman for the first out of the inning. An audible sigh was followed by a raucous uproar from the stands. One might have thought we were playing in the World Series.

After that, Jacob settled in. And he threw gas. He threw as hard as I'd ever seen him throw. The catcher's mitt popped with one of the sweetest sounds on earth. The sun was shining, and I could smell grass and dirt. My boy was playing baseball. He would proceed to sit down the next two batters, striking them out back-to-back on eight pitches. He hurled a masterful nine pitch inning when I never even thought he'd step on the diamond—like it never even happened.

He finished the game, and he finished the season, playing as hard as he ever played. Every time he took a ground ball off the body, every time he dove for a ball, every time he slid into a base or crashed the plate, the Westminster baseball moms would rise to their feet, hands over their mouths or on their heads saying, "Get up, Jake. C'mon Buddy." Each time it happened, Sandy would tell me, "Dear God, I can't take this!" They'd been through the journey with us, and they were as invested as we were. Sandy threatened to dress him in bubble wrap.

Jake didn't just finish the baseball season, he also finished the school year. All told, from the time he got sick in late November until he returned in April, Jacob had missed nearly half of his pivotal eighth grade year. We feared he might need to repeat the grade and then have to endure watching all his friends move on to high school without him. We accepted that it was a likely consequence of his lengthy illness. He was a strong student though. He always got As and Bs on his report cards.

He'd worked diligently in making up all the missed schoolwork in the hospital. When the final grades were tallied, not only did he not need to repeat the eighth grade as we feared, but he finished with flying colors. In fact, he received the Presidential Award for Academic Excellence. Furthermore, his final grades secured his acceptance at Montachusett Regional Vocational Technical School.

Alethea and I attended the Overlook Middle School graduation ceremony with beaming pride and emotional hearts. The gymnasium was packed. As the names of the graduates were announced, thoughts cluttered my mind as I recounted where we'd been over the past weeks and months and how blessed we were to be sitting where we were sitting at that very moment.

I looked across the gymnasium at my son seated amongst his friends and classmates, clapping and cheering as each name was read, and as the students made their walk to accept the diploma that would send them on to high school. I thanked God for giving this to me. I thanked Him for not taking our son.

When Jacob's name was called, the building rocked. There was a standing ovation as he made his graduation walk. I had to sit down because I couldn't completely contain my emotion. I still hated for people to see me with my tears in my eyes. I was still overcome by people being so wonderful. I would never get used to that. They cheered and cheered. People came and hugged me and Alethea, or they just laid a soft hand on our shoulder as they walked past, as if to say, "We have children too. God bless you."

They were touching moments, and in many ways, it all felt like the closing of a book. My heart was full. For the first time, it dawned on me that it wasn't only Jacob who'd been healed. Our family was back together in all its perfect imperfection. There were sports and bills and work. There were chores and arguments and issues. There were messes, accidents, and injuries. There was normalcy. There was thankfulness. I loved my wife and my kids more than I ever had, and I didn't let either a sunset or a rainstorm go by without a smile. The world was a beautiful place. I looked at people differently than I had before. Jacob's saga would move farther and farther backward in time, but it would never leave our hearts.

Perhaps Jacob's illness had no particular meaning. Perhaps his healing had no significance. Maybe the spike in his oxygen level when we prayed over him in Worcester was an anomaly. Maybe the all-encompassing peace I experienced when I wrote the letter to him in Boston was just fatigue. Perhaps the Gift of Tears was an illusion or a placebo. It's possible that Jacob's terrific recovery, though unusual, was entirely explainable. Maybe having no measurable deficit in his mind or body after suffering massive oxygen deprivation for weeks was a stroke of luck. Maybe the goodness in the hearts of people was a fluke. Maybe faith and prayer played no part in anything, and maybe they're really nothing but an imaginary crutch for the weak.

On the other hand, maybe everything does mean more than we can possibly imagine. Perhaps there is real power in prayer. Maybe the attack on Jake's lungs and his suffering and healing were purposefully meant to serve as a conduit for love, peace, and hope. Maybe the Lord really did use Jacob to gather souls together. Perhaps it's the very ability to wonder about the mysterious things in our hearts, the things that are unknowable, that ultimately defines us as the beings we are. Perhaps the greatest mystery in life is the mystery of life itself.

EPILOGUE

I am both blessed and haunted by Jacob's illness, his healing, and his recovery. It sneaks up on me when I least expect it. A memory, a sight, a sound, or a smell brings it all rushing back. Even as I've resumed the daily grind, not a day goes by that I don't think of it in some capacity. Tears creep up on me. Smiles suddenly appear. Thankfulness abounds. There are times I'm convinced that the emotional ride will continue for all my days.

In many ways it's difficult for me to reconcile what occurred. I often struggle with why my boy was saved when so many others aren't. There are times I feel guilty about rejoicing in our miracle and our triumph. At times, the guilt weighs heavily on me. Just since his healing, two of my personal friends have lost children. I've had many people praise Jacob's healing and tell me they're so happy because we *deserved* it. Although I know the aim of their sentiment, such a thought makes me recoil.

In my humble estimation, attempting to assess what anyone in this life deserves is a pointless undertaking. Trying to gauge what anyone deserves or doesn't deserve is judgmental and inconsequential, and it will change nothing.

Jacob's survival is something outside of me, something I concede that I will never comprehend. I am a man of faith, but I've never thought of myself as a godly man, nor I fear, will I ever be mistaken for one. Indeed, I regard myself as the very least of the

Lord's servants. I'm double-minded and weak. I'm often selfish, pre-disposed to wrath, sometimes foul-mouthed, envious, and materialistic, and my mind has harbored egregiously depraved thoughts. I am no more or less deserving of anything than the next man. Any thought that I deserved to have my child survive should be quickly dispatched. I know several people who have lost a child and certainly none of them deserved it.

My heart aches for those who have a lost a child a hundred times more than it ever did before. When I inventory the things of my heart I realize that, in Jacob's suffering, I was completely shattered. I merely glimpsed the level of anguish that comes with losing a child, and yet I was shaken to the core. I imagine that the measure of the heartache borne by parents who bury a child cannot ever be described and is likely the deepest sorrow one could ever experience in this life.

One could argue that there was no real point in Jacob's survival. After all, he'll eventually die, as will we all. In that regard, one could wonder what the point is for anything at all. Truly, the answers to such questions are elusive. I like to think that God doesn't waste anything though. Maybe the Lord will use Jacob for something glorious on earth or perhaps in heaven. My senses tell me that I likely may never know, at least in this life, and neither may Jake. My belief that Jacob is loved by God, though, provides me with ample comfort.

I've always looked for answers. Life itself, it seems to me, is a perpetual search for answers. We seek answers, often ignoring the fact that knowing an answer doesn't necessarily change a situation. Knowing the *why* is often of little consequence to the *what*. Two people on a sinking ship are in identical positions, even if one knows why the ship is sinking and the other doesn't. Still, we seek the why.

Answers, like many things, can be illusions and distractions. Knowing why Jacob was dying would have done precisely nothing for me, or him, at the time. Knowing why he was healed would likely only result in further mystery. Not knowing answers, it appears, is the cornerstone of faith. Where Jacob's heart will go now is known only to God.

Much will never be known in this lifetime. Still, to me, the options appear definitive. We were either specially created, or we weren't. There is either purpose or there isn't. It's entirely possible, I suppose, that the conclusions drawn when I was a young boy are correct, and none of it matters anyway. But maybe, just maybe, it all really does matter.

While I don't expect the story of a sick boy from a small town in Massachusetts to change anything in the world, it's my hope that it might in some way provide a simple message of love and hope, or that it might somehow serve as a lighthouse in someone else's storm. It might also serve as a reminder that, in more ways than we may realize, when we open our hearts to the goodness that exists in our fellow man, and when we open them up to the wonder of miracles and the mystery of faith, we may one day find, in one way or another for each and every one of us, that the healing is here.

Who shall separate us from the love of Christ? Shall trouble or hardship or persecution or famine or nakedness or sword? No, in all these things we are more than conquerors through Him who loved us.
Romans 8:35,37

Keith and Alethea live in Gardner, Massachusetts,
with Jacob, Nicholas, Isabella, and Samuel.
Perfectly imperfect. Thankful and blessed.

Jacob swings a bat every chance he gets.

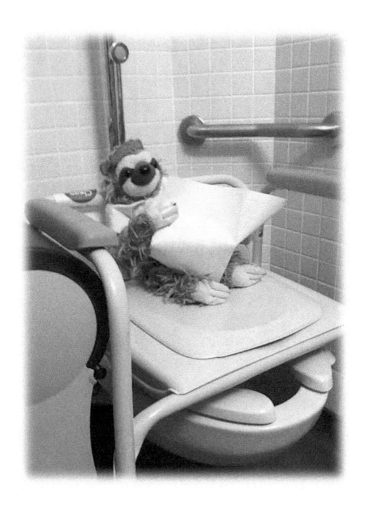

…and Bernie is still searching for a little privacy.